Lecturing
and Explaining

George Brown

Methuen

First published in 1978 by
Methuen & Co. Ltd
11 New Fetter Lane, London EC4P 4EE
© 1978 George Brown
Filmset in Great Britain by
Northumberland Press Ltd, Gateshead, Tyne and Wear
Printed by
Richard Clay (The Chaucer Press) Ltd, Bungay Suffolk

ISBN 0 416 70910 9 (hardbound)
ISBN 0 416 70920 6 (paperback)

for Sheila

Contents

Contents ix

Preface and acknowledgements

This book is based upon workshops which I have given on explaining and lecturing in universities and polytechnics in this country and abroad. As far as possible, I have kept closely to the format and methods of presentation in these workshops. Hence the style of the book is oral rather than literary. Most books avoid the use of the imperative and of 'I', 'you', etc. I use them here to cut down on circumlocutions and on space. For similar reasons, I apologise to women readers for so often referring to a lecturer as 'he', a lecturer's work as 'his', and so on.

I should like to thank my friends and colleagues at the Universities of Nottingham and Loughborough and the Open University for trying out the activities and ideas in this book. Grateful acknowledgements are given to Donald Bligh, Professor Ruth Beard, Professor Lewis Elton, Professor D. Layton, Mr A. Laing, the Nuffield Foundation, Phil Bradbury and *The Times Higher Education Supplement* for permission to quote extracts. My thanks also go to Diana Simons and Patrick Connell for battling with my typescript and to David Mack of Loughborough University, to Kif Matheson of the University of East Anglia and to John Armstrong for reading and commenting upon it. A special word of thanks is given to Sheila Armstrong for her help, encouragement and support. The book is due as much to her encouragement as it is to my efforts. Hence it is dedicated to her.

Prologue

If you believe that anybody with an advanced knowledge of their subject can teach in higher education without any form of training to do so, then this book is not for you. For it takes as its starting point that this sort of teaching is a complex, challenging activity, and that all of us, as lecturers, should from time to time reflect on our methods, and consider ways of refining our existing skills and of developing new ones.

This book focuses upon explaining and lecturing. These are two of the most common activities of lecturers. We explain ideas, processes, procedures and rationales to students, colleagues and technical staff. Yet rarely do we think about the business of explaining.

Most of us give some lectures every week during term and perhaps some during vacations. By the time we retire most of us will have given over 8,000. However, as lecturers we seldom have the opportunity to consider either the rich variety of possible lecturing methods or the most efficient ways of preparing lectures and the most effective ways of delivering them. Even more rarely can we try out activities with small groups of colleagues which are designed to help us reflect on and modify our strategies of explaining and lecturing.

This book provides some such opportunities. It can be used in at least four ways. First, you may simply read it. This will take most people less than three hours and your time will be well spent since you will learn of various strategies and activities that you can use, and of relevant research about them. But reading on its own will not necessarily help you, the reader, to modify your own methods. Secondly, you can read the book and try out some of the activities on your own or with small groups of students. This will give you some practice, and you (and your students) are likely to benefit from the experience. Thirdly, you can use parts of the book as the basis for one-day or two-day courses with groups of interested colleagues from your own discipline and, preferably, others.

2 Prologue

This will enable you to share experiences. In so doing you will learn through discussion and watching your colleagues at work as well as from the activities, hints and suggestions given here. If you do decide to arrange such a course, then you may find that the suggestions in Appendix C are helpful.

The fourth way of using the book is for organising or participating in a fully fledged course on explaining and lecturing in which all the activities here are tackled systematically. The course would take about 100 hours, and could be full-time or part-time. In my view, two days of intensive work followed by half-day sessions throughout the year and a final two-day session would probably be the most effective arrangement. Participants would then have time to learn new approaches, to reflect on them, to apply them in their teaching and to bring to the course their new experiences and problems.

The book is divided into six Units. The first two are concerned with explaining, the next three with preparing, giving and evaluating lectures, and the last Unit with learning from them.

Explaining is at the heart of teaching in higher education just as its obverse, understanding, is at the heart of learning. We give explanations in tutorials, seminars, practical classes, field courses and lectures. So explanations are important in their own right. They also, however, contain many of the elements of lectures. Explanations, like lectures, require pre-liminary analysis and preparation, and careful attention to structure and presentation.

Explanations are a representative sample of verbal and non-verbal lecturing behaviour, and their analysis and evaluation provide many pointers for analysing and evaluating lectures. Thus, explaining is not only important in itself, but its study and practice also lay the foundations for the Units on lecturing.

The Units on lecturing in their turn provide a foundation for the brief, but important, final one. This outlines some of the basic processes of learning from lectures and provides some activities, hints and suggestions about helping students to improve this.

Each of the Units contains activities designed to develop the skills involved in explaining and lecturing. A file of activities and notes should be kept by active users of the book. Some of the activities are for private study, some are for use in lectures and the bulk of them are for small groups. Many of these small-group activities require video-recording and playback facilities. The small-group activities are best carried out by participants drawn from different disciplines so that they can all experience, explore and examine different approaches to teaching and learning. Some of the activities are difficult, but rather than rationalise, try them and discuss them with colleagues who have also tried them. If you still consider them irrelevant to the work of a lecturer, feel free to write to me. Better still, invent activities which you think are more relevant and try them out, as I have done.

The activities and structure of the book rest upon some basic educational principles.

(1) It is usually better to proceed from the simple to the complex, from the concrete to the abstract.
(2) Active reading results in greater learning than passive reading.
(3) Analysis and practice with informed feedback improves skills and increases understanding.
(4) Understanding of teaching and learning comes from practice, observation, analytical discussion, awareness of one's own actions and of the reactions of others – and reading.

These principles are simple to understand but often difficult to put into practice. Similarly, you may find the ideas, hints and suggestions in this book relatively easy to comprehend. The test is: can you translate them into action?

ACTIVITY 1 – What is good teaching in higher education?

This is best carried out by groups of five or six members of a lecture or discussion class, and is useful as a first activity on a course. It may start you thinking about teaching, including your own. The first part may be attempted by anyone reading this book on their own.

Imagine you are at a meeting of parents and schoolteachers who are discussing the characteristics of good teaching. Suddenly the chairman turns to you and says: 'You work in higher education. I wonder if you could tell us briefly what good teaching in higher education is.' Spend three minutes jotting down notes about what you would say.

Draw lots or toss coins to choose two people to give their presentations. After the presentations everyone, including the presenters, should comment briefly on them and describe their own notes. Compare openings, endings and order of presentation as well as the content. Did the notes and presentations answer the chairman's question?

The groups should then spend ten minutes discussing and deciding on the most important characteristics of good teaching in higher education. After this, a member from each should present his group's list of them on the blackboard. The whole class should then take five minutes trying to decide which are the three most important. On completing this part of the activity, members of the class should turn to page 106, where they will find a further question to be considered by the small groups in the class.

Unit One – On explaining

This Unit and the next are concerned with aspects of explaining. Having read it and carried out the activities suggested, you should be able to distinguish between different types of explanation and to identify the important characteristics of good and bad explanations. But first, carry out Activity 2.

ACTIVITY 2 – On explaining

You will need a camera, video playback system and adequate audio-visual facilities (blackboard, etc.).

Select a *small* topic or an idea from one of the courses you will be teaching during the coming year. Prepare a brief, lucid, interesting explanation of it to give to a small group of lecturers who you may assume are highly intelligent but know little or nothing about the topic. Present the explanation *in four minutes*. You may use blackboard, slide projector, overhead projector or other audiovisual aids. At the end of the third minute you will receive a signal that you have only one minute left.

Some examples of explanations which have been given and understood appear on pages 6–7. Read through them and the notes on organisation before beginning the activity.

Notes on Activity 2

1 Most of you will be very skilled at explaining ideas to people more knowledgeable than yourselves. This activity is to help you to tackle the problems of explaining ideas to people who are less knowledgeable than you. It also introduces you to the main points of

explaining, to lecturing and to the problems of selecting, organising and timing explanations. An error of one minute in four minutes may be trivial, but it is equivalent to one hour in four hours or to one term in four. Talking more quickly to speed up your transmitting of information does not guarantee that the information is processed more quickly by the recipients.

2 Activity 2 is concerned only with preparing and giving an explanation; Activity 9 deals with viewing, discussing and analysing explanations. For the video-recording and discussion sessions you should work in groups of, preferably, six lecturers drawn from different disciplines with group discussion leaders who have had some experience of videotape and microteaching techniques. Details about the organisation of video-recording and the role of leader are given in Appendices A and B.

3 In the video-recording session each lecturer must play four roles: (a) lecturer; (b) time-keeper; (c) camera operator; and (d) student. The lecturer presents his explanation. The time-keeper times it, and signals at the end of the third minute by ringing a bell or banging once on the desk. He does this again at the end of the fourth minute, and the lecturer must then complete his sentence and stop. The camera operator should concentrate primarily on the lecturer but should also take shots of the 'students'. He should include close-ups of the lecturer that highlight gestures and facial expressions. There should also be shots of the blackboard or overhead transparencies. Those of overhead transparencies are rarely satisfactory, but don't worry – the quality of the explanation is more important than that of the video-recording. The 'students' must take notes, since these are important for discussing the explanation. Note-taking also tests whether the explanation was understandable to the 'students'; it reminds them of the task of learning and note-taking in lectures.

4 Allow about one hour to practice with the equipment and to video-record six four-minute explanations. Check that the equipment is working beforehand and again after the first explanation. Ensure that the microphone is well placed (small clip-on microphones are better than standing ones).

5 Do not view the video-recording until you have read the next sections of this Unit and the instructions given in Activity 9.

Examples of actual four-minute explanations given by lecturers
1 How local anaesthetics work.
2 How penicillin kills bacteria.

3 The basic principles of fruit pest control
   (how can fruit pests be controlled?).
4 Why rotate crops?
5 What are the fundamental principles of meat marketing?
6 What is job evaluation?
7 The basic concepts of accountancy.
8 What is microeconomics?
9 What is entropy?
10 How do we see?
11 What is cholesterol?
12 Why is D.N.A. important?
13 What is tragedy?
14 What are the main elements of symbolism?
15 Why was Dr Johnson so prejudiced against Jonathan Swift?
16 What were the doctrines of the Catholic revivalist movement in the
   nineteenth century?
17 Is history just facts?
18 The transmission of electricity.
19 Stress and strain in beams.
20 What are algorithms?
21 How are limits defined?
22 A simple instruction to a computer.
23 The basic concepts of architecture.
24 Architecture and community life.

What is explaining?

Put simply, explaining is giving understanding to someone else (see Thyne, 1963). There are many levels and forms of understanding and consequently many levels and forms of explaining. The precise relationship between them has bedevilled philosophers for centuries. No solution to this problem is likely before you give your next lecture. So, for the moment, stick to the working definition: *explaining is giving understanding to someone else*.

It follows from this that the act of explaining involves an explainer, 'explainees' and something to be explained. The last may be thought of as a problem, and thus the explanation has to present or draw out a series of linked statements, each of which are understood by the explainees and which together lead to its solution. These linked statements can be labelled 'keys', since they unlock understanding. A key may be a generalisation or a principle, or it may contain example, illustration or perhaps a qualification of the main principle. When the problem is complex there may be a running summary of key statements during the explanation as well as a final summary.

Here is a very simple example which illustrates the use of keys. It is based upon the aetiology of dental caries or – 'Why do sweets rot teeth?'

The answer one might give to a six-year-old is:

'Sweets contain sugar. Sugar rots teeth.'

To a nine-year-old one might say:

'Sweets contain sugar. Sugar feeds bacteria. Bacteria rot teeth.'

To an eleven-year-old one might say:

'Sweets contain sugar. Sugar feeds bacteria. Excessive bacteria attack the teeth.'

And to a thirteen-year-old:

'Sweets contain sugars. The complex sugars are broken down into simpler sugars. This process increases the growth of bacteria, particularly in crevices in the teeth where bits of sweets are lodged. The excess bacteria attack the enamel and dentine of teeth.'

The keys are the nub of explaining. But, as you can see, if an explanation is to be understood, then the explainer has not only to consider the problem to be explained but also the knowledge and characteristics of the explainees. What is appropriate for postgraduate biochemists as an explanation of the structure of D.N.A. is unlikely to be so for first-year biology students. When my nine-year-old son asked me, 'What's King Lear about?' the explanation I gave was different from one I might attempt with advanced students. Truth may or may not be absolute but explanations are always relative and, at best, only asymptotic. There is no such thing as *the* good explanation. What is 'good' for one group of students may not be good for another. The quality of an explanation depends on the degree of understanding it generates in the explainees. For different groups of explainees, the keys of the explanation, and the explanation itself, will be different – although the *use* of keys and other strategies may not be.

Similarly when trying to explain the nature of a problem, such as the relationship between truth and meaning, one uses keys. The task of the explainer is *explaining the problem*. The latter itself may either have no solution or, perhaps, several unsatisfactory solutions, but at least it can be understood. (To say that the problem cannot be understood unless it has been solved implies a very narrow definition of understanding). This point is emphasised since much of high-level teaching is concerned with explaining not the solution but the nature of problems.

Explaining in teaching is usually intentional. The explainer usually intends to explain something – though he may deal with points he did not intend to explain and he may, alas, sometimes not explain what he intended to. The explainees, we may assume for the moment, are people striving to understand. Understanding and explaining are both active processes: the explainees (students) must strive to connect what they know with what the explainer is saying or demonstrating, and the explainer (lecturer) must try to make such connections clear and meaningful. How to do this is dealt with later in this Unit. But before tackling these problems it may be profitable to consider briefly various types of explanations, and some of the research on explaining.

Types of explanation

There are three main types of explanation – the 'interpretive', the 'descriptive' and the 'reason-giving'. They approximate to the questions 'What?', 'How?' and 'Why?'. Interpretative explanations specify the central meaning of a term or statement or they clarify an issue. Examples are answers to the questions, 'What is a novel?', 'What is a biome?', 'What is enantriopy?'. Descriptive explanations describe processes, structures and procedures such as, 'How does a bicycle pump work?', 'How is a sentence used in logic?', 'How is sulphuric acid made?' Reason-giving explanations involve principles or generalisations, motives, obligations or values, and include causes (though most philosophers prefer to distinguish causes and reasons). Examples of reason-giving explanations are answers to the questions, 'Why are some people cleverer than others?', 'Why am I reading this book?', 'Why do people pay income tax?', 'Why is Shakespeare a greater writer than Harold Robbins?', 'Why did this fuse blow?'

These types of explanation are the main ones used in teaching (Ennis, 1969), though they are not the only ones (see Swift, 1961; Hempel, 1965; Smith and Meux, 1970). However, they do have the merit of being accessible and useful. Of course a particular explanation may involve all three types. Thus in explaining how a bill becomes a law one may want to describe the process, give reasons for it and perhaps define certain key terms. One may have to decide which type of explanation should be the first in a sequence. One could proceed from formal interpretation to description and then end with reasons, or one could begin by describing the structure or process, or one could begin with reasons. The important point is to be clear what you are doing – and why.

ACTIVITY 3 – Sorting out explanations

Which of the following require predominantly an interpretative, descriptive or reason-giving explanation (answers on page 106).

1 What is the meaning of the term 'monarchy'?
2 What is a thunderstorm?
3 Explain how a university is organised.
4 Explain how sulphuric acid is manufactured.
5 Explain how an electrical spark crosses a gap.
6 Why does dough rise?
7 What is the differential of 2x?
8 Why did you do/not do a Ph.D.?
9 Why are spiders not insects?
10 How was penicillin discovered?
11 Why do trees have roots?
12 How do fish make sounds?
13 The explanation you gave in Activity 2.
14 Why reason-giving explanations are easier to identify than descriptive or interpretative explanations.
15 What is explaining?

'Good' explaining

If explaining is the giving of understanding, then to be 'good' it must be valid in the context in which it is used, and it must be understood by the explainees. These being the necessary conditions, a 'good' explanation may not be as elegant as the explainer would like it to be but this is less important than the appearance of clear structure to the explainees. For an explanation to be understood, it must be attended to. It is partly the responsibility of the explainees to attend, but the explainer must ensure that his explanation appears sufficiently worthwhile and interesting for them to do so. Good explanations are, therefore, clearly structured and interesting (obviously, poor or inadequate explanations are confusing and boring).

These suggestions are common-sense but they also agree with the findings of researchers who have examined explanatory teaching (Gage, 1972;

Dunkin and Biddle, 1974; Turney *et al.*, 1975) or who have obtained students' reactions to various lecturing styles (Flood-Page, 1974, reviews some of these studies).

However, clarity of structure and interest are complex notions. Most people would agree that they are important, but problems arise when one begins to probe what they are and whether they can be taught. Let us look briefly at two sets of studies which explored this area.

The first of these were carried out by Gage and his associates (Gage, 1972). Over forty teachers were asked to teach fifteen-minute lessons based on reports on Thailand and Yugoslavia. Sixteen- to seventeen-year-old pupils were given intelligence and achievement (knowledge) tests and asked to react to the teaching styles. The lessons were video-recorded and rated by independent observers, and the transcripts were analysed using specially devised codes and rating schedules. These procedures enabled the researchers to relate various aspects of teaching style to pupil learning, to pupil reactions and to independent observers' ratings. 'Good' explainers scored relatively highly throughout. The major findings were as follows.

Emphatic gestures and movements, relatively short simple sentences and the use of prepositional phrases discriminated the 'good' from the 'poor' explainers. Good explainers used pauses more appropriately, employed the blackboard to indicate essential points, varied their speed of delivery and made some friendly personal references to the class or its members or to themselves. Good explanations usually involved task-orientation statements such as 'Now, let's look closely at ...'; they contained sentences which stated problems clearly and had a high proportion of nouns rather than pronouns such as 'it' or 'they'. Successful explanations contained signposts such as 'There are three main areas. First ...' They also contained a higher proportion of statements linking various elements of the explanation, such as 'So far we have looked at ... Now ...' Gage found that 'ineffective' explanations used several vague phrases such as 'Well – mm – er – all of this can ...', 'not very', 'sort of', 'kind of', 'pretty much', 'and so on', 'maybe that's kind of wrong'. (Incidentally the average length of these fifteen-minute lessons, including pupil talk, was 1,892 words.)

These studies prompted me to try an experimental course with the help of newly appointed lecturers. The first and last task of each of those who completed a two-day training programme in explaining was video-taped and rated by independent observers. Transcripts were analysed using a System for Analysing Instructional Discourse (S.A.I.D. : Brown and Armstrong, 1977). By the end of the end of the training programme, the explanations given were clearer, more fluent, and contained fewer

irrelevant technical terms and fewer complex sentences. The final explanations had well-defined keys which were related to their topic, more
concise points, examples and summaries. The lecturers looked at their
audiences more often in the final task, they used pauses more frequently
before key points and they employed gestures and verbal emphatics
('Now ...', 'So ...') more appropriately.

These findings suggest that elements of clear structure and interesting
presentation can be identified and, more important, that people can be
trained to be better at explaining. This is not to say that everyone can
become a gifted explainer of deep problems, but that one can, with
effort, improve. Unit Two is designed to help prepare, give and analyse
explanations. The next activity is designed for thinking about the structure
of explanations.

ACTIVITY 4 – The structure of explanations

This is best carried out in groups of five or six in a lecture or discussion class. The groups should compare their analyses.

Read through the two tape transcripts of four-minute explanations
given below. Each is divided into keys which are marked by a line
drawn across the page. Decide which of the two explanations is the
better and why.

Then reread each explanation. Try to decide what question the
explainer claimed he was explaining, and what question each key
actually explained. Set out the questions that he claimed he was
explaining and the ones he did explain in each of his keys. Then
examine the links between the keys and the stated questions. A suggested answer is on page 107.

TWO TAPESCRIPTS OF EXPLANATIONS

(1) Er – the – the title of my talk today is why nude mice are important
to biologists.
O.K.

Well, the thymus as most of you probably know is – er – a large – er
– organ that's located in the – em – upper part of the chest, it's
referred to as a lymphoid organ because most of the cell-cells processed
by the organ – most of the constituent cells in this – in the thymus are
lymphacytes – a specific cell type. Its importance lies in the fact that

lymphoid cells processed by this – by this organ – erm – are cells which control the mechanism of graft rejection – this is important in transplantation. Erm – they also have a specific role in immune – er – responses – erm – and the role here is one of control – it's the thymacytes, the lymphoid cells rising from this organ which determine the pattern of an immune response.

Now, one way of studying the importance of such an organ is to remove it and to see what happens in its absence so the surgical ablation or thymectomy as it's known in this particular instance has become quite a widespread procedure by [tape indistinct]. What happens is the thymus is removed – this is a procedure normally combined with irradiation – er – irradiation of sufficient intensity to destroy – erm – other lymphacytes present in the body since lymphacytes are particularly sensitive to irradiation – erm – the procedure doesn't unduly effect other cell types but – erm – in particular instances where irradiation has to be given of – erm – a lethal quantity of irradiation has to be given then the – erm – problem is that the – erm – animal has then to be reconstituted with marrow cells and kept on a variety of antibiotics to prevent infection since lymphacytes have such a-a-an important role-function in – erm – in immune responses an animal deprived of these lymphacytes then has to be kept artificially to ensure its survival, by the administration of antibiotics and so on.

Such a mouse, anyway, is known as an immunologically deprived animal and it's an extremely valuable – erm – it's an extremely valuable – erm – animal to the biologists because it provides a sort of tool whereby the role of other cell types can be assessed. You've destroyed the lymphacytes in – in this particular animal you can then re-inject other – erm – specific cell types and see how they function in – when various stimuli are given to them. Organs, for instance can be – erm – transplanted back into the animal and their role can be assessed in the absence of other interfering factors.

So where does the nude mouse come into all this?
Well, in 1966 – erm – Flanagan first described a creature – 'The nude mouse is a homozygous recessive condition' and I think one ought to explain here using the blackboard, erm – the nude condition – erm – is governed by a single gene and since each gene is – is – is represented by two [tape indistinct] in each cell of the body you have three possible combinations. You have a d– a plus, plus combination [writes on board] this is known as the wild type.

(2) The title of my talk is why nude mice are important to biologists. The term the 'nude mouse' is used to describe a strain of mouse which arose by mutation from normal laboratory mice – um. It's a condition which is characterised by two main features. These are, first of all, absence of hair hence the term the 'nude mouse' and the second feature is the absence of a thymus, and it's the second property, the absence of a thymus, which is the subject of my talk.

Now, the basic point is going to be summarised on this first table.

So, there are two conditions possible, either the thymus is present or it's absent. Thymus present, a naturally occurring condition, leads to an ability to respond. (Perhaps I should stand on this side.) The absence of a thymus which either can be experimentally induced or it can occur naturally in the nude mouse leads to inability to respond immunologically. The question then rephrased is why is the absence of a thymus a useful condition and the answer – um – simply that animals without a thymus cannot respond immunologically and therefore such animals can be injected with foreign cells – um – and the role and the function of these cells can then be studied without the interference of immune response.

Second table then once again summarises this main, this – um – this statement of mine. No thymus results in no immune response therefore there is no interference from the immune response, hence injected cells can survive and can be studied. A very useful experimental situation.

Going back to the first table – um – the last point which I want to make is that the natural condition, i.e. the nude mouse, is preferable to the experimental condition – um – because in order to achieve the experimental condition complex surgery is involved. This needs to be followed by prolonged drug treatment and such a combination – um – is highly lethal to the animals resulting in mortality of – um – experimental groups.

So, to summarise then, the nude mouse is an important – um – is important to biologists because – um – first of all it's easy to obtain relative to the experimentally induced condition and since it doesn't have a thymus it's a useful animal because it doesn't respond immunologically and it's this last condition which is in much demand in biological research.

Summary

In this Unit you have been involved in giving explanations, observing them and evaluating them. You have been introduced to various types of explanation and to some important features of good ones. The final activity required you to apply what you had read, and what you already knew, to a problem based on tapescripts. In tackling it you may have become aware of the importance of order, structure and presentation in other people's explanations. In the next Unit you will have an opportunity to analyse your own explanatory processes.

Unit Two – The business of explaining

Some people explain aptly, getting to the heart of the matter with just the right terminology, examples and organisation of ideas. Others get us and themselves all mixed up, use terms beyond our level of comprehension, draw inept analogies, and even employ concepts and principles that cannot be understood without an understanding of the very thing being explained.   (Gage, 1972)

In this Unit you will be exploring ways of preparing, giving and analysing explanations and you will be introduced to more elements of presentation and structure. The final section deals with spontaneous explanations – the ones for which you are asked unexpectedly and which you agree to give; this may happen in lectures, seminars, problem-solving classes, practicals or in unscheduled meetings with students. This final section will enable you to practise spontaneous explaining and to apply the skills which you will have been using earlier.

Explaining ideas to students can be a challenging task. They may not see connections which are so obvious to the explainer that he does not mention them. They may not share his assumptions or may not have the technical vocabulary needed for understanding the explanations. To complicate matters further, part of a lecturer's task is to initiate students in the language and assumptions of the subject. Communicating ideas involves more than just knowing about them.

The activities in this Unit are designed to help you improve your explaining to people less knowledgeable than yourself. You may find some of the activities difficult but please do not skip them because they are the foundations of later work on lecturing – and they may also help you to give better explanations when you are teaching small groups. The hints, suggestions and guidelines on explaining are based upon the researches and reviews of Borg (1975), Dunkin and Biddle (1974), Miltz (1971), Rosenshine (1970, 1971), Turney *et al.* (1975) and Wright and Nuthall (1972).

These researches reveal the importance of preparation, presentation and structure in the task of explaining; attention to these details almost always yields better results – as measured by observers' ratings and by measures of student learning.

Preparing and designing explanations

This section, like much of the book, is unashamedly prescriptive. It sets out seven steps in preparing and designing explanations which are obvious when stated, and which have been found useful by lecturers, teachers and postgraduate students (Brown, 1978[a]). All the steps are important but the first three steps are crucial:

1 Decide precisely what you are going to explain.
2 Identify the hidden variables.
3 Pick out the main points – and their relationship.

It is not enough to decide that you are going to 'explain' a topic such as 'Stresses and strains in beams'. You must also decide whether you are going to explain 'What are stresses and strains?' or 'How are stresses and strains caused?' or 'Why do beams break?' or whatever else. When the question or questions have been formulated precisely you can begin to look for the hidden variables in them. For example, hidden in the question, 'How are stresses and strains caused?', is the notion of loads and their effects. Once the hidden variables have been identified, it is usually possible to pick out the main relationships. Since steps (2) and (3) are difficult, I suggest you try the following activity before reading all seven.

ACTIVITY 5 – Taking steps

This activity may be carried out individually, in pairs or in small groups. In a lecture or discussion class it is best to use pairs who then compare their answers with other pairs.

Find the hidden variables and pick out the main points to be made in brief explanations of the following topics to a group of intelligent people.

1 How to make scrambled egg on toast.
2 How does grass grow?
3 How does an increase in the price of oil affect a nation's economy?
4 What are the main characteristics of plays?

5 What are the main differences between men and women?
6 What counts as good teaching in higher education?
7 Why do trees die?
8 Why are some people more successful than others in the same jobs?
9 Why do nations sometimes wage war?
10 Stresses and strains in the lives of lecturers.

See pages 107–8 for comments and suggestions.

PREPARING AN EXPLANATION

Step 1
(a) Decide precisely what you want to explain to your peer group. This is best done by asking yourself simple questions about the topic, such as:

What is ...?, Why is ...?, How does ...?,
How are ...?, Why do ...?, Is ...?

(b) Then ask yourself:

What might a group of intelligent people find interesting about the topic?
What do you think they should know about the topic?

Then put your decision in the form of a simple question such as:

How do local anaesthetics work?
What is tragedy?

These procedures focus your attention sharply on what you want to explain, they remind you that you are explaining to a specific group of people and they provide you with hints on how to explain the particular point.

Step 2 – Find the hidden variables
Underline the key words in your question and *set out* the relationship between them. If you cannot do this you cannot answer it. Often the relationship is not direct, but contains hidden variables as in the simple example given earlier ('Why do sweets rot teeth?') Almost all types of explanation involve a search for the hidden variables.

Step 3 – State the key points
When you have located the hidden variables you should be able to select
and state the key points. This is also a very useful procedure for preparing
lectures. Each major section of a lecture should yield a key point, and the
summary at the end should contain all of them.

DESIGNING AN EXPLANATION

The key points provide you with the understanding necessary for giving
your explanation to others. Often lecturers teach a topic better the
second time because the first time they are not sure what the key points
are – usually they have not consciously sought them out. Now that you know
the key points, and by implication which points to omit, you can begin
translating your explanation into terms which are likely to be meaningful
and interesting.

For your first attempt I suggest you use the following approach: a
lead-in (orientation), keys and a summary. Each key contains statements of
key points, perhaps examples, illustrations and analogies, *important* elaborations and qualifications, and restatements of key points. The explanation should end with a summary of the main points and perhaps a
conclusion.

Not all keys need contain examples, qualifications or restatements, but
remember that what is obvious to you may not be obvious to a learner.
It is not necessary for every explanation to begin with a definition or
interpretation: sometimes it is worth beginning with a concrete example.

Step 4 – Design the keys
Write down the problem in question form. Then for each key:

(a) *Express the key principle in a simple pithy statement.* Use a minimum
of technical terms and avoid unnecessarily complex sentences. Useful
openings to the first key are 'Put simply ...', 'Put very briefly ...', 'The
essential point is ...'. Useful openings to the subsequent keys are: 'Now
the next point is ...', 'Let's look now at the second ingredient (feature,
aspect ...)'. Then if you think it necessary, as it usually is:

(b) *Choose one or two apt examples or illustrations.* These should be
brief and unambiguous. Illustrations (including pictures and simple diagrams), helpful analogies, metaphors and hand movements may be used to
convey the message. The hands can sometimes make a point more
effectively than words.

(c) *Give any major qualifications or elaborations.* Begin these with such phrases as 'So far I've described the main points ...', 'Now some of you might have realised that there are exceptions (snags, problems, difficulties). The main exception is ...', 'Now [pause] let's probe a little deeper'. These phrases mark the openings of the qualifications you may wish to give or the exceptions or vague cases which do not easily fit the key statements. Remember to give only the main qualifications and elaborations, and to leave out information which is not absolutely essential.

(d) *Restatement and extension of key principle*. If possible restate the key principle in a slightly extended form and in different words. The latter probably increase the chance of you being understood – and of you understanding! Often a change of words or word order can trigger off the meaning.

Step 5 – Summarise the main points you have made
Bring together the main points and come to a conclusion, which should be your answer to the problem posed. Useful openings are: 'Let's now look at the points covered ...', 'To sum up then ...'. Useful openings to a conclusion are: 'So there you have it ...', 'So we can say ...'. 'So it seems that ...'. These again act as markers. Summaries are crucial for effective explaining.

Step 6 – Design the lead-in (orientation)
It may seem odd to design the lead-in after you have designed the whole of the explanation. But this will enable you to design a good one that will direct the attention of the explainees to what you want to explain. This implies that you need to motivate the group as well as inform them. If you do not know what your explanation contains, then clearly you cannot do this. The lead-in to the explanation is important since if you do not gain and hold the attention of the explainees, they may not hear or see, let alone understand, your explanation.

Try to devise a lead-in which will capture their interest as well as be relevant to what you want to explain. You may also have to use it to refresh the memories of your audience: 'Some of you may remember....' Some useful ideas for lead-ins are:

1 Begin with a reference to the explainees' experience or to yourself, e.g. 'Most of you probably did history at school and you may think that history is just a set of facts. What I want to do in the next four minutes is show that history is much more than this.'
2 Begin with a question, e.g. 'Have you ever thought what ...?'

3 Ask a provocative question.
4 Begin with a brief anecdote.
5 Show an unusual object or picture.

Step 7 – Write out your design
Set out your plan in this order. Leave a five-centimetre margin for extra
notes or points which may occur to you between now and when you give
the explanation. Do not put down every word you intend to utter even
if you feel a little nervous at the prospect of explaining, but do indicate
the main points and the links and check that the question that you intend
to explain is explained by the keys and summary.

(a) Question to be explained.
(b) Orientation.
(c) Keys.
(d) Summary.

These seven steps in preparing and designing explanations are based on
common-sense buttressed by research findings. Wright and Nuttall (1972)
have shown that orientations and summaries are important for both learning and interest and that qualifications and elaborations should follow the
main points, not precede them. Bores often begin with substantial
elaborations and qualifications. Rosenshine (1971) and Miltz (1971) have
both demonstrated that clear statements of principles and apt examples are
important. Other findings are cited by Dunkin and Biddle (1974).

The seven steps will help you to structure clearly any explanation that
you give. Eventually you will be able to shed them except for particularly
difficult topics. But even if you do, bear in mind that explaining is giving
understanding to other people, so you have to decide clearly what is to be
explained and consider to whom.

ACTIVITY 6 – Opening an explanation

This activity may be carried out individually, in pairs, in groups of
five or in a lecture or discussion class. I use it as a small-group
activity within a class.

Before going on to the section on giving explanations you might
like to read the openings of two explanations transcribed from tape
and given below. Decide in what ways, if any, they can be improved.
Compare your suggestions with those of other participants on the
course or readers of this book.

Two non-opening keys

(1) This morning I am going to explain the dental formula. The dental formula is based on bilateral symmetry of the human mouth. Well, it's not exactly bilateral symmetry, not at least in the mathematico-geometrical sense but only in a sort of statistical sense. The underlying principle of the dental formula idea is generalisable across other species but it is clearly more apposite for mammals, particularly mammals with highly symmetrical bone structures.

In your mouth you have teeth and these teeth are either incisors, canine or dog teeth, or molars. You have the same number of each of these three types in each quadrant of your mouth, if you have a full set that is. Now, you have two incisors, three molars, two canines. We don't actually have them in that order. The order is incisors, canines, molars for each quadrant. So the formula is. . . .

(2) Last – er – week or – er – rather – um – er – last time some of us – er – met I talked about meaning – er – truth and understanding. They are – er – difficult concepts [pauses, looks towards heaven for inspiration]. Yes, I think they can be regarded as – er – concepts. Well, – er – I'm not going to be talking about them to – er – day. What I – em – want to do is – er – look at or rather into a complicated and – er – neglected topic which is related in – um – various ways to – er – what I was saying last week. It is a topic which you – er – has practical relevance and by practical I mean it would be useful if – er – several people knew about what it entailed if only because – er – of its negative aspects. I – er – don't suppose that I will be – er – adding anything new to the debate and I'm not – um – proposing to deal with the – er – exhaust, I mean the – er – topic exhaustively. Well, anyway not to – er – my satisfaction. . . .

Well – er – let's look at explaining then and what we – er – mean when we say someone has explained something.

Giving explanations

Good explanations are like this author's favourite swimsuits – neat, brief, appealing, covering the essential features, yet suggesting other delights in store. In more prosaic language they are well-structured and they generate interest in their subject matter. In the preparation and design phases I mentioned the importance of apt and interesting examples and of taking into account the needs and perceptions of the explainees. The main emphasis was on the structure of explanations, because well-structured ones yield better recall and learning. However, clear well-structured explanations are not enough since the presentation may at the same time be dull and dreary. Enthusiasm for and interest in the subject you are teaching are also important ingredients. Let me say at once that I am not advocating that you emulate the manic enthusiasm of some television science correspondents, nor am I suggesting that you should adopt the fixed eye and quavering tones of an evangelist. I am suggesting that if you wish to communicate ideas successfully to a group of people, then there are certain guidelines to follow.

CONVEYING INTEREST AND ENTHUSIASM

The face, the voice, the hands, movement and stillness, and silence, these are what we use to convey interest and enthusiasm. It follows from this that the face must be seen, the voice must be heard, the hands must be used, and stillness and silence observed. All of these are part of the fascinating topic of bodily communication which Argyle and his co-workers have promoted (Argyle, 1967, 1970, 1975). Non-verbal and extra-verbal cues convey meanings of their own – the look of determination, the grunt of disgust. They also modify the verbal messages being given. The meaning of the sentence 'That is very interesting' changes if a different word is emphasised: '*That* is very interesting' or 'That is *very* interesting.' The tone of the voice may convey interest or boredom. When the phrase is coupled with a stare, then its meaning changes even more radically.

Interest and enthusiasm are not easily lured into a psychological definition but they are basically concerned with changing the patterns of stimulation of the learner so that his attention is gained and held. Lecturers and teachers who can achieve this are usually rated high on interest and enthusiasm (Rosenshine, 1970), which are one of the three sets of characteristics particularly valued by students and pupils (Ryans, 1961). The other two are warmth, and systematic, businesslike behaviour.

Just as changes in stimulation are important constituents of interesting teaching, so its absence is the hallmark of the bore who goes on and on in the same old way. Most of you will have attended at least one boring lecture! If you analyse that lecturer's non-verbal cues you will probably find that they were few; that he rarely changed his facial expression; that there were no gestures and often a surfeit of ums and ers; that he rarely moved and if he did, it was with resignation; and that he spoke in a dull flat monotonous voice. Most of us, even the dullest, can improve if we pay attention to the following points.

The face and eyes

The mouth, nose, forehead, chin and eyes can all convey meaning and control interaction. Pursing the lips indicates impatience, raising the eyebrows shows astonishment and opening the eyes wide conveys enthusiasm or astonishment. Eye movements and contact are an effective way of conveying interest. If you lean forward a little and look at a person, this is a signal of interest. If you are talking when you do this, then he will usually respond non-verbally – providing he's looking at you! If you stare hard at a person whilst you are talking it is difficult for him to interrupt. If you do not look at a person whilst you are talking, this is often read as a signal of lack of interest or fear. Incidentally, if you are nervous about looking at people in a lecture audience, at least you can pretend to do so. This hint helped a particularly shy lecturer to acquire confidence in his lecturing technique. After trying it in a lecture, some of his students told him he had improved, and subsequently he *did* improve. The hint gave him confidence in himself and it was this that led to his improvement.

Eye movement and contact not only convey enthusiasm and interest, they also enable you to monitor whether you are being understood. You will find yourself registering 'That puzzled her', 'She looks unconvinced', 'He got the point', 'He's not interested', and this helps you to improve your explaining. Lastly, but by no means least, you are more likely to be heard if you look at the audience than if you look at the floor, ceiling or your notes.

The voice

To be listened to, one has to be heard. Inaudibility may be due to a number of factors. Like other musical instruments the voice has functioning parts. First the breath passes through the vocal chords and produces a complex note. The note then passes through the pharynx, the mouth and the nose. Each of these acts as a resonator. A good tone quality depends on the balanced coordination of these resonators. A predominance of pharynx resonance produces a muffled chesty sound, excessive mouth resonance, a harsh authoritarian tone and too much nasal resonance a thin reedy voice.

ACTIVITY 7 – Reading aloud

This activity may be done privately, but is best carried out in small groups.

Read a short poem or a paragraph from a newspaper in a muffled voice, a harsh authoritarian voice, and a thin reedy voice.

Discussion of Activity 7
This activity may have produced some tensions in your throat, jaws, nose and mouth. These are likely to develop spontaneously when you are nervous. To minimise them you have to be confident about your material and relaxed about talking to a group of people. Even then, in the early stages of lecturing you are likely to suffer from some throat tension.

Audibility is also often lost by slurring, swallowing or clipping words. Speakers of English usually drop their voices at the end of sentences and a crucial point may go unheard. Beginners also tend to speak much too quickly or, less often, too slowly, whereas variations in speed of delivery are more effective, as are the use of pauses and markers such as 'Now [pause]', 'Well [pause]', 'So there you have it [pause]'. Remember that not only have you to be heard but also to be listened to and understood. When lecturing, you should remember, too, that students usually need or expect to take notes from what you say, so that it is important that you express yourself interestingly as well as clearly. Helpful exercises on improving diction and expression may be found in Gohdin, Mannen and Dodding (1970) and Robinson and Becker (1970).

The hands
Our hands often give unintentional signals of our emotional state. You may have found yourself gripping the telephone very tightly when speaking to someone you dislike. Picking one's nails, opening and closing one's hands, playing with a pen or looking at one's hands are usually interpreted by onlookers as signals of nervousness and may be off-putting to them, be they colleagues or students.

One can use the hands intentionally to convey meanings. The raised finger or hand may emphasise a point, the palm facing outwards can signal a qualification to the main point. 'But ...' with a stretching out of the hand can indicate a request to agree. The following are examples of using the hands to emphasise a point: 'It was this notion of Maxwell's that lifted [lecturer lifts hands] the level of conceptualisation and experiments in electromagnetism.' 'But let us be clear what Leavis was saying [lecturer removes spectacles, looks at audience] ...'. 'But, as you know, bacteria grow and split, grow and split [lecturer places finger and thumb of each hand together, opens them slowly to simulate a circle, separates the hands and produces two circles, one with each finger and thumb].'

Movement and stillness
As an undergraduate I had a lecturer who walked about 1,000 metres per

hour along the front of the theatre and he spoke at about 50 words per minute. It was wryly observed that he was 'pedestrian' in his approach and soul-destroying in his delivery. Some movement is desirable during long discourses since this produces change of stimulation in the learners and so retains their attention. This point is taken up again in the Units on lecturing. If you do wish to move occasionally, then make sure that you are still when making an important point. Passing shots are hard to get in lectures as well as tennis.

It is also important to be still at the beginning of a lecture or explanation. This is the first step in gaining people's attention. You should pause, look slowly around the lecture class or group and wait until they appear to be attending. Sometimes young lecturers have management problems in lectures simply because they do not attempt to gain attention. By pausing and looking around, you signal that you expect to be listened to and are confident that you will be.

Silence
The first time you pause and look around an audience you may find the experience agonising. Time passes slowly when you are waiting to speak. When you pause to look at your notes you may feel that the audience is waiting for you. In fact they are more likely to be relieved or hardly to notice.

Silence is an important device for gaining attention. If you suddenly stop in the middle of a sentence, people look up to see what has happened. If you pause before a point, you signal that it is important – whether it is or not. If you pause after a question, you signal that you are expecting an answer – but it does not always follow that you will get one. If you deliberately pause for a couple of seconds, this usually means disapproval, and if you pause for more than thirty seconds without indicating why, you will almost certainly receive signals of disapproval.

New lecturers tend to be afraid of pauses and silences and rush to fill them with extra statements or questions. More experienced lecturers use silence to gain and hold attention.

ACTIVITY 8 – Reading aloud and listening

Read the last two paragraphs aloud twice: first quickly without any pauses, and then at a varied speed with pauses inserted appropriately to emphasise what you think are important and interesting points. If possible, use a tape recorder and listen to your own voice.

This section has been largely concerned with hints which will help you to convey interest and enthusiasm. They are useful for lecturing (and seminar teaching) as well as for explaining. Further hints will be given in sub-sequent Units. The next activity is concerned with observing your own explanation. Before doing so, you should read the hints given below and look through the guide for analysing explanations in fig. 1.

Hints on giving explanations

Actions to take	*What to avoid*
Pause, look around the group and wait until they are ready	Starting when only one or two are listening
Make your opening remarks in a friendly, personal way	
Look at members of the group and watch their reactions	Staring hard at the ceiling and floor
Use some gestures to emphasise points	Semaphore
If you want to, move about a little	Marathon walk
When you use visual aids, make sure they can be seen	Showing your back – even if it's your best feature
Use connecting links	Confusing asides and irrelevancies
Keep your explanations (keys) and examples brief and interesting.	Avoid excessive qualifications, highly technical words and complex sentences
Pause before making an important point or asking a question and look at the audience	Dropping your voice and examining your toes when you are saying something important
Try to vary the pace of delivery	Avoid uniformly slow or high-speed deliveries

PART 1

Put a ring round the response which most closely describes your views on the following features of the explanation.

Name of explainer .... Topic ....

<u>Orientation</u>   <u>Responses</u>

1. The opening gained and held   1. Yes   No   Not observed
    attention.
2. The opening remarks established   2. Yes   No   Not observed
    rapport.
3. The opening remarks indicated what   3. Yes   No   Not observed
    you intended to explain.

<u>The Keys</u>

4. The key points were clearly   4. Yes   No   Not observed
    expressed.
5. The examples were apt.   5. Yes   No   Not observed
6. The examples were interesting.   6. Yes   No   Not observed
7. The qualifications were clearly   7. Yes   No   Not observed
    stated.
8. The summaries of each key were   8. Yes   No   Not observed
    clear.
9. The beginning and end of the keys   9. Yes   No   Not observed
    were clearly indicated.

<u>The Summary</u>

10. The summary brought together the   10. Yes   No   Not observed
     main points.
11. The conclusions were clearly   11. Yes   No   Not observed
     stated.

PART 2

Now rate the explainer on each of the following items:

    6 = Outstanding for a beginning lecturer
    5 = Very good
    4 = Good
    3 = Fairly competent
    2 = Weak
    1 = Poor

Put a ring round the number which most closely describes your views.

1. Use of gestures to emphasise and illustrate   1.   6 5 4 3 2 1
    points.
2. Use of eye contact.   2.   6 5 4 3 2 1
3. Use of audio-visual aids.   3.   6 5 4 3 2 1
4. Verbal fluency.   4.   6 5 4 3 2 1
5. Appropriateness of vocabulary.   5.   6 5 4 3 2 1
6. Use of pauses and silences.   6.   6 5 4 3 2 1
7. Absence of vagueness.   7.   6 5 4 3 2 1
8. The clarity of the organisation of the   8.   6 5 4 3 2 1
    explanation.
9. The interest of its presentation   9.   6 5 4 3 2 1
10. Its degree of intelligibility to the   10.   6 5 4 3 2 1
    explainees. (Was the explanation
    understood?)

PART 3

Jot down a few comments on how you might modify and improve the
explanation:

....

....

....

....

....

....

....

....

Fig. 1   Explanation guide

Looking at explaining

ACTIVITY 9 – Looking at your explanation

First use the hints above and fig. 1 as the basis for a discussion Then view and discuss the video-recording made in Activity 2.

The person who gave the explanation should be the first to make comments on it. His colleagues should then be invited to add theirs. The note-takers should state which points they understood and which they found confusing. Good as well as poor features of the explanations should be highlighted. The primary purpose of the viewing and discussion is to help the explainer to analyse and improve his explanatory skills. (Notes on the role of the discussion leader are given in Appendix B.) At the end of the discussion each member of the group and the explainer should complete an explanation guide (fig. 1). The explainer should keep these for use in later activities in this Unit.

If this is the first time that you have seen yourself on videotape, you will be fascinated by your mannerisms, body shape and movements as well as by your explaining and the reactions of the explainees. Follow your natural inclinations to look closely at yourself. Whilst looking try to decide which mannerisms are socially acceptable and which you think should be changed. Stroking one's chin when considering a point is socially acceptable, shoving a finger up your nose is not. When commenting after viewing, tell your colleagues what you thought of your mannerisms. Usually they are less important than you think.

Note: To save time in Activity 10 you may audio-record each of the four-minute explanations directly from the video-recorder.

Discussion of Activities 2 and 9

Activity 2 may have been mildly nerve-racking even though you were working with cooperative peers. They are not likely to have suffered psychological damage from your first fumbling attempt. Before giving the explanation you may have thought that four minutes are not sufficient for explaining anything; that four minutes of viewing cannot tell you anything about yourself; that you could not teach your peers because you were not aware how much they knew about the topic; that you did not know what to do, despite the instructions; that the camera would affect your performance; that the view of yourself on the screen was not true to life. You may add further rationalisations to the list – and then consider the task of lecturing to 100 first-year students.

Activity 2 was deliberately simplified and artificial in order to enable you to focus sharply upon a particular task: explaining. Most explanations of a point take less than four minutes. At an annual conference of French medical researchers, each director is only allowed five minutes (plus a one-page handout) to give his annual report on the research activities of his team.

Some people ask: 'Why did we do Activity 2 before we read about preparing and giving explanations?' The answer is: You are more likely to gain an understanding of the processes of structuring and giving explanations after you have tried to give one. Otherwise, it is easy to dismiss the steps and hints on explaining as trivial. It is less easy to dismiss them when you have tried and know that your explanation was far from perfect. The activity has alerted you to the processes of explaining so that the act of reading about it has become more meaningful.

A four-minute sample of teaching behaviour yields considerable information. Indeed, it can seem a long time when viewing a videotape. The camera may cause anxiety, but so does the presence of 100 undergraduates. The video-recording does give you the opportunity to see yourself and analyse your performance whereas a normal lecture class does not. The view from a video-recording may not be as accurate as you would like – but it is a view. In teaching one rarely has enough time to explain all aspects of a topic or theme, and attempts to cover rapidly *all* the ground do not lay the foundations of understanding. It is better to begin by selecting and highlighting the main features. The essence of teaching is the promotion of understanding, not of logorrhoea.

Observing explanations, like looking at many modern paintings, requires training and experience to increase appreciation and sensitivity. What we see is determined partly by what we are looking at and partly by our expectations, attitudes, values and knowledge.

Each of the three parts of the guide for analysing explanations (fig. 1) uses a different system for recording observations. Each of these methods may be used for analysing, lecturing or small-group teaching – although, of course, the items one chooses to record will be different. Part 1 is an example of a simple sign system in which one indicates the presence or absence of a particular teaching move in the four-minute interval; sign systems may be used with any time interval from a few seconds to a few minutes. Part 2 is a rating schedule with a six-point scale. Even-point scales force one to indicate whether one's rating was 'good' or 'bad', whereas odd-point scales allow an escape into neutrality. The first six items on this scale are specific elements of explaining and the last four deal with global impressions of clarity, interest and intelligibility. Part 3 asks you for free-ranging responses to the explanation. (See Stubbs and Delamont (1976), Rosenshine and Furst (1973), Eggleston and Galton (1975) for discussion of ways of observing teaching.)

All of these have their strengths and weaknesses. The sign systems enable one to map only the main features. But by using them more frequently, say every 30 seconds, it is possible to map in more detail. The rating schedule highlights particular elements or impressions but much information is lost. The free-ranging response gives a global report in which tiny critical incidents and events may be noted which the structured systems may not catch. It is also worth remembering that free-ranging responses are the most subjective, and personal values may distort what one sees and selects for one's report.

Looking into your explanations

So far we have looked at explaining. We now go beyond the perceived reality to underlying structures and meanings – in other words, to structural analysis. Analysis is at the heart of scientific endeavour and of rigorous literary criticism; the next activities require a blend of both scientific and literary skills. You will be analysing the tapescript of your explanation.

ACTIVITY 10 – Transcribing your explanation

Use the audio-recording made during Activity 9 for most of this task and the video-recording to check on non-verbal details. Transcribe fully your four-minute explanation. With a five-centimetre margin on each side of the paper, transcribe all the words and the extra-verbal cues such as ums and ahs, and insert brief descriptions of non-verbal aspects such as [wrote on board], [pointed], [gestured emphatically], [dropped notes], [laughter], [glares], [silence]. This activity may take about one hour. Do not attempt to write down every gesture and movement – just the main ones.

If it is the first time you have transcribed a tape you may be surprised at the number of extra-verbal cues, the complexity of your sentences and the hesitations at unexpected points. You should now

compare the design of your explanation with what you actually said
and did. Closing the gap between intention and action is an important
part of training.

The transcript gives you an accurate verbal picture of your explanation. It may lack the movement and flow of the video-
recording but it has the merit of allowing you to probe deeply into
what you did. This is not an easy task, so be prepared to observe,
search, compare and think during the next activities.

The next task is to analyse your tapescript. The method of analysis is
based upon S.A.I.D., the System for Analysing Instructional Discourse,
which was developed initially by Sheila Armstrong in order to study
explaining in secondary-school science lessons. It grew out of her studies
of Ennis (1969) Smith and Meux (1970), Bellack *et al.* (1966) and the
British linguists Sinclair and Coulthard (1975). Since then Sheila Armstrong and I have used it for analysing explanations, lectures and seminars
(Brown and Armstrong, 1977).

The analysis may, for your purposes, be divided into three parts: firstly,
the identification of the keys; secondly, the identification of key questions
or statements; and thirdly, the identification of various elements of the
explanation, such as hesitations and stumbles, vague phrases, inappropriate vocabulary, rephrasing, and emphatic markers such as '*Now*', '*So*',
'*Let's look at*', which indicate the beginning or end of important points
or keys. The procedures are set out in the next activity. (The tapescripts used in Activity 4 were divided into keys.)

ACTIVITY 11 – Analysing your explanation

1 Read through the tapescript and underline the opening key
  (orientation), the keys and the summary key. To identify the
  keys look for markers such as 'Let's look now ...', 'Now ...', and
  for distinct shifts in the subject matter.
2 Whilst you are doing this, try to identify the key statement(s)
  within each key and to decide what question the key was
  designed to answer. Underline the key statements and note the
  key questions on a separate sheet. Decide what problem or
  question you, the explainer, claimed to be explaining and note
  this.
3 Count the number of hesitations and stumbles (h), vague
  phrases (v), inappropriate vocabulary (i), rephrasing (r) and

emphatic markers (m). Inappropriate vocabulary is such as is unlikely to be understood and/or does not contribute to the explanation. Rephrasing is, in small measure, useful. Emphatic markers at the beginning and end of keys or before or after key statements are also useful; but at other points they may be distracting.

4 Set out your analysis of the explanation in the order:
  a Question to be explained.
  b Opening key question (and statements).
  c Key questions.
  d Summary key.
  e Frequency counts of hesitations, etc.
  f General impressions of the quality (or lack of it) of the explanation.
  g Examine the analysis to ascertain whether the explanation clearly emphasised the problem and, if you are dissatisfied with the structure and emphases, how you might change them.

5 Exchange tapescripts and analyses with a member of the group, read through his tapescript and see whether you agree with his main analysis. Discuss and compare them with each other.

Explaining revisited

By now you should be fairly confident of your ability to prepare, design, observe and analyse explanations. The next task is to try another four-minute explanation. If you were pleased with the structure and presentation of your first explanation, it is best to try another topic. If you were dissatisfied, try the same topic but sharpen up the structure and, if you were highly dissatisfied, then either try the same topic or change topics.

ACTIVITY 12 – Explaining revisited

Redesign the explanation given in Activity 2 or design and give another one. Follow the instructions in Activity 2 but reverse the order in which members of the group present their explanations. It is important for the 'students' to take notes as they did then. Whilst listening to the explanation and immediately afterwards, they should try to answer the questions in fig. 2. The explainer should attempt the same questions during the viewing session.

Try to answer the following questions whilst listening to the explanation (*in vivo*) and immediately afterwards or, if it is your own
explanation, during the viewing session and immediately afterwards.

1. What were the key points? Were they clear?   (Yes/No)

        Opening Key
        Key 1   (Yes/No)
        Key 2   (Yes/No)
        Key 3   (Yes/No)
        Key 4   (Yes/No)
        Key n   (Yes/No)
        Summary Key

2. What was the central question being explained? What major type
    of explanation was called for (Interpretative, Descriptive or
    Reason-giving)?

3. What type of explanatory processes were used in each major key
    excluding the orientation and summary? Were they clear?

    Descriptive (How)   Interpretative (What)   Reason-giving (Why)

    Indicate the type for each key and your estimate of its clarity.

	Was it clear?	Yes/No
Opening Key		
Key 1	.. .. ..	.. ..
Key 2	.. .. ..	.. ..
Key 3	.. .. ..	.. ..
Key 4	.. .. ..	.. ..
Key n	.. .. ..	.. ..
Summary Key	.. .. ..	.. ..

4. Was the explanation in session 3 better than in session 1?

            Yes / No / Marginally yes / Marginally no

Fig. 2   Guidelines for explaining revisited

ACTIVITY 13 – Explaining reviewed

View and discuss the video-recordings made in Activity 12, following the procedures indicated in Activity 9. The discussion
should focus on the structure of the explanation, the keys should be
examined in relation to the central question being explained, and the
links between keys should also be examined. Suggestions, if necessary, on ways of improving the structure of the explanation should
be given by the explainer and by members of the group. Each
member of the group should complete the guide for analysing explanations (fig. 1). These together with their answers to fig. 2 should
be given to the explainer, who should read them and form his own
opinion of his attempts.

Spontaneous explaining

So far we have looked at planned explanations and ways of improving them. This is a large part of a lecturer's explanatory work, but it is not the whole. Often we are asked unexpected questions. We can dismiss them during a lecture with a brusque 'I don't answer questions in lectures' or we can, if it is appropriate, try to answer them spontaneously. In seminars, tutorials and practicals it is not usually possible or desirable to avoid on-the-spot explanations. This section provides some guidelines and activities which will help you to cope with spontaneous explaining. Needless to say, the more experience you have of preparing and giving explanations, the more likely you are to become better at spontaneous explaining.

GIVING SPONTANEOUS EXPLANATIONS

1 To give an explanation spontaneously or otherwise you have to be clear what you are trying to explain. 'Could you explain the Wars of the Roses to us?' could mean: describe the events in the Wars of the Roses (descriptive explanation), give the main reasons for the Wars of the Roses (reason-giving explanation), or what were the Wars of the Roses (interpretative explanation). Hence your first step is to clarify what is to be explained.

2 You next have to establish what the questioner already knows about the topic. If he is familiar with the royal families of Lancaster and York, you can proceed from this to an explanation of the clarified question. This second step – discovering what the questioner already knows – also helps to clarify the question.

3 You now have to analyse the question posed and determine the hidden variables or keys in the explanation and the order in which to present it. You can begin with a generalisation and work towards examples, or you can proceed from a concrete example to general principles. The latter is probably the best for most descriptive explanations and for some reason-giving explanations.

4 Choose simple models and analogies to explain the problem. Then if you think it necessary, indicate where the model or the analogy does not closely fit.

These are general hints which you should bear in mind when carrying out the following activities, the first of which is largely concerned with analysing the hidden variables in a question. All the activities are best carried out in groups of six drawn from different disciplines.

ACTIVITY 14 – Hot-seat explaining, I

Each of the questions below should be written on a separate card. Read through them, locate the hidden variables and think out simple explanations that could be used in a discussion with someone who knows little or nothing about the topics. Spend fifteen minutes doing this.

Sit in a circle. One person in the group should now ask any other to answer any one of the questions. Allow only two minutes per question. The explainer may ask any questions he likes but this is part of the two minutes allotted to him. He may pass the question to the person on his left. If it is passed all the way round the group back to the questioner, then he must answer it. (Not everybody is expected to produce perfect explanations of all the questions.) When the explainer has answered the question, the rest of the group should each give him a mark out of 2 (2 = splendid; 1 = all right; 0 = inadequate). After receiving these marks, the explainer should ask another member to provide an explanation of one of the questions. Continue until everyone has answered two questions. Spend five minutes discussing what the activity has taught you about explaining. Which explanations seemed the best – and why?

The questions are:

1 Why do trees have roots?
2 Why does a person die if he stays under water?
3 Why does salt disappear when you put it in water?
4 Why do some women students take the Pill?
5 Are university lecturers agents of the State? Give reasons for your answer.
6 Is explaining an art or a science? Give reasons.
7 What is pure about pure mathematics?
8 What is marketing research?
9 What is the difference between sociology and history?
10 How do economists define poverty?
11 What is geography about?
12 What is low-temperature physics?
13 What are polyamines?
14 What is Common Law?
15 What do zoologists do?
16 What is the difference between psychologists and psychiatrists?
17 How does water circulate in a central-heating system?

18 How do chameleons change colour?
19 How do you become a university lecturer?
20 Was Joyce a novelist or poet?
21 What is symbolism?

Obviously you may add to, or subtract from, this list if you wish. But keep to about twenty questions so that there is always a chance element.

ACTIVITY 15 – Hot-seat explaining, II

Activity 14 may have seemed tough even though it allowed some time for preparing explanations. This one is perhaps even tougher. Here, each member of the group is in the hot seat for five minutes.

Before playing this game, establish what areas of research or teaching each person is involved in but do not ask him to clarify terms or concepts. Spend about ten minutes jotting down questions you wish to ask him about his subject. Draw lots to decide the order of people for the hot seat. Sit in a circle.

The three people immediately opposite the person in the hot seat may each fire three questions at him about any aspect of his research or teaching (the explainer may ask clarifying questions). The other two note the questions and answers and give each explanatory answer a score (2 = splendid; 1 = all right; 0 = inadequate). The explainer may pass – any pass scores −1. At the end of *five minutes* the note-takers give their scores and comments to him. The next member of the group is then in the hot seat.

Continue until everyone has been in the hot seat. Compare scores and discuss what you have learnt about explaining and questioning from this activity. Note that the explainers' scores are partly determined by the questioners.

If Activity 15 seems too daunting you may, instead, like to try the following one, which is concerned with explaining and understanding.

ACTIVITY 16 – Hot-seat explaining, III

Establish which areas of research and teaching each member of the group is involved in. Divide into pairs: the pairs should be those who know *least* about each other's subject. Each pair should together discuss their respective research and/or teaching for a total of five minutes. At the end of the five minutes the group of six should again form a circle. Then each person should report what his partner has told him (at this point the partner should not comment). Go round the circle but make sure that two partners do not report consecutively. At the end of this session each person should make any corrections to the report that he thinks are necessary and comment briefly on its accuracy. The group should then discuss briefly what they have learned about explaining, questioning and reporting from the activity.

The accuracy of the report is, of course, partly determined by the explanatory skill of the explainer and the listening and comprehension skills of the explainee. The activity involves explaining, questioning, listening, understanding, summarising and reporting. It may be used at the beginning of a course on explaining as a warm-up exercise and as a way of helping a group to get to know each other. Perhaps it should be renamed 'ice-breaker' rather than 'hot seat'.

Summary – the end of explaining

This Unit has been concerned with the task of explaining. We explain ideas, problems, processes and procedures in lectures. We are often called upon to explain in seminars, tutorials and practicals and we may also have to explain to committees, secretaries, technicians and clients. Explaining is at the heart of teaching in higher education just as its obverse, understanding, is at the heart of learning.

By now you should be able to distinguish different types of explanation, you should be able to prepare and give clear explanations, and to observe and analyse explanatory skills and explanations critically. At the same time you should have learnt many of the more central skills of lecturing and small-group teaching and have re-experienced the problems of listening, understanding and note-taking. You have also been involved in small-group learning situations in which you taught and learned from your peers both formally and informally.

All of this is valuable not only in its own right but also as a preparation for lecturing and other forms of teaching. But the major activities that you have carried out on explaining are not the same as the activities of lecturing. Lecturing differs from explaining in at least three main ways – time, size of group, and group capabilities. In one-hour lectures you have rather more flexibility than in four-minute explanations. In the latter you might use an approach which over one hour would become boring. The size of lecture groups means that you may have to speak more clearly, to look around a larger audience and perhaps to be better organised than for four-minute explanations. The groups to which you lecture are likely to have a much wider range of ability than your colleagues, and perhaps more knowledge. Thus, you may have to consider more carefully the levels at which you pitch your lectures. As a rough guide, it is best to consider the middle group, with occasional forays either to interest the brighter students or help the less able ones.

Unit Three – Learning about lecturing

'The decrying of the wholesale use of lectures is probably justified. The wholesale decrying of the use of lecturing is just as certainly not justified.' (Spence, 1928)

Lectures are for the benefit of students. They are predominantly oral methods of giving information, generating understanding and creating interest. Without interest, attention is lost and so there can be little understanding. Without information there is nothing to be understood. The task of lecturing is therefore threefold; it is rather more than the delivery of slabs of facts or loose chippings of ideas.

The threefold task of lecturing causes anxiety to many lecturers who have not been trained in communication skills. Students' reactions to lecture methods of teaching are also, sometimes, cool, though this may be partly due to over-use of lecture methods and to the scarcity of good lecturing. Researchers frequently point out that lecturing is probably not, on balance, as effective as small-group teaching for complex problem-solving or for changing attitudes. But for imparting ideas and information, lecturing is about as effective as other methods of teaching, (Bligh, 1972; Bligh *et al.*, 1975; Costin, 1972; McCleish, 1976). However, even these results, of course, depend on the quality of the discussion or lecture.

What some researchers do not point out is that lectures are an economical way of teaching which has been in use for some 2,500 years. There are many methods of lecturing and many possible uses of them. They are unlikely to wither away because of the findings of us researchers. Indeed lectures are likely to increase as staff–student ratios get worse. Rather than bemoaning the deficiencies of lectures one should seek ways of improving their effectiveness.

The topics of this Unit are anxieties about lecturing, how students learn from lectures, the basic skills of lecturing and the use of lecturing space. By reading it and carrying out the activities, you should be able to recall and report your own anxieties; you should be able to state the main processes involved in learning from lectures; you should find it possible to formulate a list of basic lecturing skills; and you will have some practice in some of them.

Anxieties of lecturing

Lecturing probably causes more anxiety amongst lecturers than any other form of teaching (see, for example, King, 1973), particularly amongst young lecturers. Anxiety diminishes as one becomes more experienced – but it is likely to re-emerge at the beginning of an academic year or when giving a special lecture. Perhaps, however, some anxiety feelings are necessary in striving to be successful; indeed they may be the motivating force in mastery.

When anxiety floods us, we react in one of two different ways. We erect defences against it or we try to combat it. These strategies are like the psychoanalytical notions of defending and coping. Common defences are:

Denial.   Not so much denial as non-acknowledgement. Examples: refusing to look at a lecture audience, reading every word from lecture notes, hiding behind a strategically placed briefcase.

Projection.   Attributing to students our own inadequacies. 'These students don't understand' = 'I don't understand.'

Rationalisation.   Dubious reasons for doubtful actions: 'I'm not wasting my time on preparing lectures for first-year students. Anyway I'm going to the theatre tonight.'

Intellectualisation. The use of intellectual powers to avoid decision or commitment. Examples: spending so much time on reading a topic that there is no time to prepare a lecture on it; retreating into obscurity in the hope that incomprehensibility will be equated with wisdom; ritual concentration of facts without indicating what is important.

Substitution.   Space filling – substituting dubious activities for lecturing. Examples: waffle – talking around a point; flannel – waffle plus an intention to mislead.

Reaction formation. Behavioural paradoxes – Doing the opposite of what is said in such a way as to imply the opposite of what is said. Examples: giving a totally disorganised lecture on the importance of organisation and structure; saying in a lecture 'Do ask any questions' in a menacing voice.

Repression. Forgetting what one does not wish to know. Example: forgetting to prepare or give a lecture class.

Unfortunately, defences wall up anxieties, and do not reduce them to a tolerable level. To reduce anxiety one has to face the problem squarely, analyse it systematically and attempt to combat it. This is 'coping', and a first step in coping is to draw out the problem. It is open to debate whether the psychoanalytical reasons given are always the reasons for various deficiencies and stances. Awareness of such matters is, however, the first step towards coping with lecturing and its anxieties.

ACTIVITY 17 – Anxieties of lecturing

This activity is best carried out in groups of five or six. It is divided into five parts.

1 Each member of the group should write down the following:
   (a) Examples of the defences which they have used or have observed in others.
   (b) A brief description of a particularly bad lecture.
   (c) A brief description of a particularly good one.
   (d) A list of their own anxieties and problems in preparing and giving lectures.
2 The members of the group should then, in turn, compare examples of each of the defences against anxiety. Everyone should indicate whether they have used or observed the examples cited by the others.
3 The descriptions of a bad lecture should then be compared and their common characteristics picked out and listed.
4 Similarly with the descriptions of a good lecture.
5 After examining the lists of good and bad characteristics the members of the group should state what aspects of lecturing and preparing lectures bring out most anxiety in them, and should compile a list of common anxieties. This may be retained and re-examined after completing the activities in this book.

How do students learn from lectures?

Students learn from lectures by listening, observing, summarising and note-taking. A hidden variable in their activities is understanding. Sometimes understanding is gained in the lecture, sometimes it emerges whilst the student is poring over his lecture notes afterwards. Fig. 3 sets out a simple schema for examining the processes of learning from lectures. It is derived from studies of human information-processing (see, for example, Lindsay and Norman, 1972).

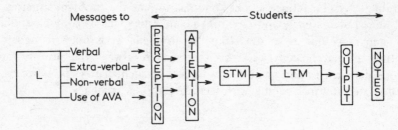

Fig. 3   Learning from lectures

A lecturer sends messages verbally, non-verbally, extra-verbally and by using audiovisual aids. The information is received, sifted and stored by the students. They also summarise the messages received and produce notes on them – this is the germ of truth in the old saying that lecturing is the transferring of notes from the lecturer's to the student's notebook without them passing through the heads of either.

The messages which the lecturer transmits are not only concerned with information. His non-verbal and extra-verbal cues may convey meaning and attitudes which highlight, qualify or distort the essential messages. The latter may be clearly structured and meaningful or they may be confused and seemingly meaningless. The messages may or may not be attended to. Attention fluctuates throughout a one-hour lecture. After twenty minutes there is a marked decline in attention followed by a peak just before the lecture ends (Johnstone and Percival, 1976; Lloyd, 1968; Maddox and Hoole, 1975). The decline is less likely to occur if the lecture includes some brief activities for students; a change of activity is, in fact, likely to renew attention.

Messages which are received by the students are filtered and stored temporarily in the short-term memory. They are forgotten after about thirty seconds if they cannot be rehearsed or cannot be transferred to the long-term memory. The latter will most readily receive messages which are related to the network of concepts and facts already stored there. The long-term memory will also store new messages which are loosely associated with existing facts and ideas. Messages that are incomprehensible are most likely to be forgotten.

→Recall of information from lectures is not notably efficient. McCleish (1968) reported that 40 per cent of the important points were recalled immediately after a lecture and only 20 per cent a week later. The loss can be reduced drastically if students study and learn (not by rote) their notes. Similar results have been reported over the past fifty years (Jones, 1923; Bassey, 1968). Similarly, note-taking from lectures is not notably efficient. In one experiment Hartley and Marshall (1974) estimated that the average amount of information noted was only 11 per cent (see also Howe, 1977). Since few students take shorthand notes – nor should they – the results of these experiments are not as surprising as they may seem, but their implications are important. If one wants students to learn from lectures and to take good notes, one has to structure one's presentation so that it is meaningful and interesting; one has to ensure that their attention is gained and sustained and that the ideas and facts presented may be readily assimilated into their existing store of knowledge and skills. One might also spend some time helping students to improve their learning from lectures (the final Unit contains some hints on this).

Students' output is not only a set of intelligible notes which may be understood and, if necessary, restructured and learned, it also contains reactions to the lecture and lecturer. These reactions are usually non-verbal signals which may be received, interpreted and perhaps acted upon by a lecturer who is not totally occupied with reading his notes or writing on a blackboard.

Perhaps more important than immediately observable output are the longer-term changes which may occur within a student. A lecture may change a student's perceptions of a work or theory, it may increase his insight and it may stimulate him to read, think and discuss ideas with others.

ACTIVITY 18 – Structure and learning

This activity is best carried out in a lecture or discussion class. The two lists should be written on separate transparencies.

   1 Spend one minute looking at the list of twenty-four nonsense syllables. Then, without looking at it, write down as many as you can in one minute.

2 Spend one minute looking at the twenty-six words in List Two. Then, without looking at it, write down as many as you can in one minute.

3 Check your answers.

4 Divide into groups of five or six and discuss briefly which list was easiest to recall and why. Itemise the reasons. Also discuss briefly the implications of the experiment for learning from lectures and itemise these. To what extent do your lectures take account of these reasons and implications?

5 The groups should then briefly compare their lists of reasons and implications. The class may also like to comment on the differences between this activity and learning from lectures.

List One: nonsense syllables

TAL	PAF	QOL
IGF	FEG	NUG
NYF	HAT	WOF
MEL	YIL	GEV
KUG	ROG	XYM
OKL	ZOK	BIS
LYF	JOM	ELG
GUF	DIT	CIN

List Two:

Minerals

Metals Rare	Common	Alloys	Stones Precious	Masonry
Gold	Aluminium	Brass	Diamond	Granite
Platinum	Copper	Bronze	Emerald	Limestone
Silver	Iron	Steel	Ruby	Marble
	Lead		Sapphire	Slate

Some basic skills of lecturing

Understanding the processes of learning from lectures provides a basis for understanding and practising the basic skills of lecturing. The experience you have gained in the Units on explaining may already have alerted you to the difficulties of note-taking and to the problems of pre-

senting and structuring brief explanations. In this section you will be
exploring some basic presentation skills in lecturing, and the structure of
lectures is the subject of Unit Four. The table below sets out a list of
basic skills that are important in lecturing, but before reading it you might
like to try producing your own one.

Your list may differ from mine. What matters is not whether it does
but the act of producing it. This makes you aware of the skills involved
in lecturing and their importance to you. Below are a few suggestions and
several activities in this area. All the activities are best carried out in
small groups. Video-recordings are not essential but analytical discussion
is. The discussion should be opened by the person who carried out the
activity, and should focus primarily upon ways of improving the skills
used in it. The group should also discuss what has been learned from
the activity. Even if you feel that your subject does not require you to
use skills in the activities, you should carry them out, since this sort of
practice may help you in unexpected ways.

Some basic skills of lecturing

1 Explaining   giving understanding, using examples and
                                 illustrations

2 Orientation   opening a lecture, introducing a topic or
                                 theme   important points at end of lecture

3 Closure   summarising themes and linking topics
                                 and themes

4 Liveliness   generating interest and enthusiasm, giving
                                 and holding attention

5 Using audiovisual aids   the effective use of blackboards, overhead
                                 projectors, slides and models   demonstrations or
                                                                  movies

6 Varying student activities

7 Giving directions   indicating how to carry out procedures or
                                 how to solve various types of problem

8 Comparing   comparing and contrasting, giving
                                 similarities and differences or advantages
                                 and disadvantages of various methods,
                                 approaches and perspectives

9 Narrating   reading from a novel, play, poem or a text
                                 to illustrate or exemplify a point of view

Note: The skills overlap. Each contributes to the main aims of lectures – giving information, understanding and interest, and each may be analysed into other components. Each skill involves intentions which may require preparation, actions which require performing and feedback which needs evaluation.

EXPLAINING AND ALLIED SKILLS

Explaining, orientation, closure and liveliness have been discussed in Units One and Two, so they will not be considered here. However you might like to try the following activity.

ACTIVITY 19 – Beginning a lecture

Read the following extract from a review and prepare a lively (or interesting) and clear opening (orientation) for a lecture based on it. Choose a title for this imaginary lecture. Give the orientation to the other members of the group in about two minutes. Video-record these if you wish and discuss them. In the discussion compare and contrast the different orientations based on the same material and how they differ from the written review.

Note: (1) The orientation should only contain the essential features, not the details of the review. (2) Similar exercises may be carried out with other reviews or short articles.

M. A. K. Halliday has long been one of the most original of British linguists. His considerations of language have always united a penetrating analysis of specific fields of language studies with a concern for the most general questions about the nature of language. This breadth of vision has gone together with a much wider range of interest than is, or was, usual in linguistics. Even in the days when syntax and phonology were the only respectable fields for a linguist, Halliday's work embraced such 'marginal' topics as stylistics and other forms of text studies. It is thus no surprise that his latest book deals with a neglected aspect of language.

Halliday has suggested that language can best be understood as fulfilling three major functions. First, there is that function of language which is concerned with representing or communicating our experience, both internal and external, and Halliday calls this the 'ideational' function of language. Second, one can consider language in terms of the positions it allots to speaker and hearer—in terms that is of the interpersonal function of language. This is the area of modality; of commands and questions. Third, there are those elements within language which function as links between one sentence and the next. These elements which bind sentences one to another are the elements which allow for the formation of texts and it is this text-forming function which Halliday calls cohesion. This book attempts to provide an account of cohesion in modern English and to investigate the very different kinds of relation which make a text cohere. In its early stages this book was the research work of Ruqaiya Hasan who developed some of Halliday's ideas but since then the text has been revised and expanded by both linguists.

USING AUDIOVISUAL AIDS

Audiovisual aids here mean any equipment or materials which a lecturer may use in a lecture. Handouts, the blackboard, overhead transparencies, models, slides, audio-recordings, video-recordings and films are examples. There is little doubt that skilful use of these aids sustains attention and improves achievement amongst secondary-school pupils (Turney *et al.*, 1975) and is also likely to be effective in higher education.

Audiovisual aids may be used as a series of props for the main points of a lecture; this is the common use for the handout or blackboard summary. Alternatively they may be explanatory devices in their own right, e.g. an overhead transparency which shows a simplified diagram of, say, a chemical process or the structure of a play. Aids can also serve to enrich lectures, e.g. short extracts from films, video-recordings or sequences of slides.

We shall not examine all the methods, problems and pitfalls of using audiovisual aids (Hall, 1975, gives a set of practical hints). However, there are a few important precautions one must take:

1 Illustrations and summaries should be simple, brief and readable from the back of the lecture class. If the illustrations are important, let the students have time to look at them and, if necessary, to copy them; if they are available in a book or journal, give details and page number. There is no need to keep speaking whilst the class are looking at illustrations.

2 Handouts should be brief and well-structured. They should contain key references and, if necessary, definitions of new terms. Lengthy handouts become substitutes for lectures, not adjuncts to them. It is probably best to give students a few minutes to read through a handout just before you begin lecturing. If a handout would pre-empt the excitement of the lecture, then give it out afterwards.

3 Slides, films, audio- and video-recordings are an effective way of interspersing a lecture and maintaining interest and attention (though excessive use may induce sleep). One must indicate clearly which features of the material should be particularly attended to. If possible, one should pose questions for the students to ask themselves during the audiovisual performance, give them an opportunity

for brief discussion of the materials, then summarise the main points and link them to the relevant parts of the lecture. These guidelines are important – without them a potentially valuable learning experience can be reduced to the level of home movies.

The two activities that follow are concerned only with the use of simple audiovisual aids.

ACTIVITY 20 – Using a prepared audiovisual aid

Select a small segment of a topic which is suitable for expressing in a simple diagram. Prepare the diagram on an overhead projector transparency or on a large sheet of paper, together with a simple explanation of it. Show and explain the diagram to the members of the group in less than four minutes. Discuss each member's presentation, particularly the clarity of the explanation and of the diagram, how well he maintained contact with the group and how his approach might be improved upon.

Note: (1) If you video-record do not use an overhead projector: the picture quality is usually too poor for this activity. (2) One way of estimating lecturer–student contact is to count the number of times a lecturer looks at his audience.

ACTIVITY 21 – Building up an audiovisual aid

Select a small segment of a topic which is suitable for expressing in a simple diagram. Prepare the diagram only in your notes together with a simple explanation of it. Draw it on a transparency, blackboard or large sheet of paper *as you give the explanation* to the group. The discussion should again be concerned with the clarity of the explanation and of the diagram and how well the lecturer maintained contact with the group. (See notes at end of Activity 20.)

THE VARYING OF STUDENT ACTIVITIES

Skilful use of audiovisual aids sustains attention and enhances learning. The same applies to the varying of student activities in a lecture. It does not follow that because you have a one-hour lecture you must always give a one-hour monologue. Indeed the work already cited on attention and memory suggests that lectures interspersed with student activities are likely to be more beneficial to the students and more interesting. What matters in lectures is, ultimately, not what the lecturer says or writes on the blackboard, but what the students learn and what encourages them to learn more.

One simple, effective method of involving students in lectures is known as 'buzz groups', which consist of brief discussions in groups of three or four students of questions or problems posed by the lecturer (alternatively, the buzz groups can invent the questions). In lecture theatres buzz groups can be formed in sections of rows. They take very little time but give students an activity and a break so that they return to listening and note-taking with renewed concentration. Buzz groups encourage students to discuss, think and offer contributions, whereas asking a question to a large audience usually results in silence. Reports from buzz groups give an immediate check on whether the students have understood the main points the lecturer has been outlining. The reports may be used as the basis for a section summary in a lecture or to introduce the next section.

Buzz groups are for brief activities. One can also use slightly larger groups for longer periods on miniature case studies or problems, plus a reporting session. In lecture theatres this can be done in sections of rows of four or five students or sections of two rows of four or five students. Those in the lower two turn round and face the upper row during discussion and then turn back for the report. In lecture rooms with light moveable furniture the students may group for the discussion. Bligh et al. (1975) give many useful hints and suggestions for varying activities in lectures.

ACTIVITY 22 – Using a buzz group

Prepare one or two questions or simple problems for use in buzz groups in one of your lectures – make sure that they are relevant to the lecture. Ask for some reports from the buzz groups, summarise the views expressed or solutions offered and, if possible, link them to the next section of the lecture. Repeat Activity 22. (Prepare another set of questions or simple problems for use in another lecture, either with the same or a different class).

Write a brief report of your observations of the reactions of the lecture classes to the use of buzz groups. Discuss these reports with a small group of five or six colleagues who are also using the technique, and note any relevant hints that emerge.

GIVING DIRECTIONS

It is obvious that directions should be clear, unambiguous and in the correct order. It is less obvious how to prepare and present them in this way. Systems analysts use decision trees, algorithms, path analyses and flow charts for clarifying and giving directions, all of which are useful but beyond the scope of this book (see Rowntree, 1974). Instead, here are two simple activities which should help you become aware of ways of improving your skills in giving directions.

ACTIVITY 23 – A game of directions

A dice or three coins plus a pack of 'task' cards are needed for this game, which is best played in groups of four. Prepare a set of twenty simple tasks which involve giving directions. Some examples of apparently simple tasks together with a set of joker cards to include in the pack of task cards are given below. The game is played by a 'director', a 'listener' and two 'onlookers'. Each person takes a turn at being director; the listener is chosen by tossing coins (odd man out) or rolling dice; the other two participants are onlookers. The director draws a card from the pack of task cards and gives directions for the task. The listener then repeats them. The two onlookers give a score out of three to the director for clarity, and a score out of three to the listener for accuracy: 3 = very good, 2 = good, 1 = all right, 0 = inadequate. The onlookers must give reasons for their scores, which should be noted. The game is then repeated with another director. There is no need to withdraw task cards from the pack because they have been tackled – in fact, there should be some improvement in the second attempt at a task within a group. After playing for about a half hour, two groups of four should form a group of eight to discuss briefly what they have learnt from the game and to prepare a list of seven practical hints for anyone who has to give a set of directions. Use this list as a checklist in the next Activity. (See also a brief comment on page 109.)

Some examples of apparently simple tasks
  (a) How to prepare scrambled eggs on hot buttered toast.
  (b) How to prepare a breakfast of coffee, toast, bacon and egg.
  (c) How to plan a dinner party.
  (d) How to set up a study group.

(e) How to play ludo.
(f) How to play knock-out whist.
(g) How to start a car.
(h) How to clean a window.
(i) How to get from your university or polytechnic to your home.
(j) How to shave your legs.

Some examples of 'jokers'

Pass left: Choose another task card and pass to the person on your left.

Pass right: Choose another task card and pass to the person on your right.

Reverse roles: You are now the listener in this task. Pass the pack of cards to the person on your left.

Onlooking: You are an onlooker, pass the pack of cards to the nearest onlooker on your right.

Choose again: Deal another three cards from the task pack and choose any one of them.

No choice: Deal another four cards. The fourth card is your task.

ACTIVITY 24 – Giving directions

This activity is best done in groups of eight.

Choose a simple practical task which you can demonstrate how to do, and can give directions on. The rest of the group can practice immediately. The task may be related to your own subject or to some everyday activity (e.g. how to set up a simple apparatus, how to read a section of a map, how to read a table, how to take a pulse reading). During each demonstration two people should act as observers and the remainder attempt to follow the directions. The observers should use the checklist compiled in Activity 23. After the demonstration they should give their evaluation. The demonstrator and the 'learners' should then suggest ways, if any, in which the directions could be improved. When everyone has carried out a demonstration, the group should summarise briefly what they have learnt about giving directions.

Note: If the activity is video-recorded the cameraman should focus on the attempts of some of the participants to carry out the task as well as on the demonstrator and his directions.

COMPARING

Comparing and contrasting two viewpoints is a complex form of explaining which requires the explainer to identify and describe essential similarities and differences. This theme is discussed briefly on page 69.

NARRATING

Reading aloud to illustrate a point is a simple yet often neglected skill. A brief, apt quotation can reinforce or exemplify a point, or can be used as an introduction to, as an example within, or as a summary of, a section of a lecture. Narrating requires clear diction, expressive speech and contact with the audience. It also involves the choice of apt quotations and the strength to resist the temptation of one's favourite passages.

Clear diction and expressiveness are the province of teachers of speech and drama, but it is not suggested that you should learn to act in order to lecture. Nonetheless, you may find the following activities help you to become aware of the quality of your diction and your range of expressiveness.

Imagine you are about to enter a lecture room of students whom you have not met before. Go outside the room, open the door, walk in and say a few introductory words to the rest of the group. Do this as if you were (a) nervous; (b) over-confident; (c) confident. The rest of the group should guess which you were doing.

ACTIVITY 25 – Diction and expressiveness

This activity may be carried out with an audio- or video-recorder, with one other person or with a small group of people. If other people are involved they should stand or sit about twenty feet away from the 'lecturer'. The listeners should note their comments on each part of the activity and report these to him when he has completed the whole thing.

(a) Say the following clearly:

1. A nice man   3. Fork handles   5. A diseased man
2. An ice man   4. Four candles   6. A deceased man

The order may be varied.

(b) Repeat a selection from the following list. Try to convey the feelings indicated. You may use non-verbal cues as well as vocal expression.

(*Sadly*)	It seems, gentlemen, that the only lesson that History teaches is that mankind does not learn from its history.
(*Confidentially*)	But, of course, these are not the only interesting features of Lawrence's work.
(*Enthusiastically*)	Now this was a truly marvellous discovery. It revealed at one stroke....
(*Dismissively*)	That, gentlemen, is trivial.
(*Enthusiastically*)	But this, gentlemen, this is almost nontrivial.
(*Questioningly, with interest*)	So then, what were the main problems facing Brunel in this project?
(*Slowly, clearly, yet with enthusiasm*)	Now there are three clearly discernible themes in Faraday's work. First ..., second ..., and third....

(c) Now repeat a selection of the following statements as if you were speaking to an audience in a way which would interest them in the subject matter. You may use non-verbal cues as well as vocal expressiveness.

1 So Pasteur concluded that there was little point in pursuing this project.

2 Leavis's views on Lawrence are well-known. His views on Milton less so. Yet it is his views on Milton which reveal more starkly his critical values.

3 So there is the proof that e to the power of $\pi\chi\iota$ equals -1. Let's stop now and examine this statement. We cannot assign a real value to e or to π. ι is another mystical number. It is the square root of -1. So we do not know what any of these symbols mean. But we do know that e to the power of $\pi\chi\iota$ equals -1. Such, gentlemen, is the power of pure mathematics.

4 So we can conclude, with Wittgenstein, that if you have truly understood what he has said then you will know that it is meaningless. Think about that. In the next lecture we will be looking at yet another aspect of Wittgenstein's work.

5 Every subject has its own language and assumptions. Medicine

is no exception. By the end of a medical course a student will have learnt approximately 80,000 new words. They may not all be part of his active vocabulary but he must be capable of quickly relearning and using them. In contrast most ordinary people have an active vocabulary of approximately 4,000 words.

6 'Lecturing may be defined as an instructional technique through which an agent presents an oral discourse on a particular subject' (Verner and Dickinson, 1968).

7 Sometimes, as George Bernard Shaw noted, we are assaulted by '... the jargon of those writers who because they never really understand what they are trying to say, cannot find familiar words for it, and are therefore compelled to invent a new language of nonsense for every book they write'.

ACTIVITY 26 – Narration

This activity is best carried out in a small group. The group should sit twenty feet from the lecturer. The proceedings may be video- or audio-recorded. On completing the activity each of the listeners should comment briefly on the lecturer's diction and expressiveness and they should suggest ways it might be improved.

Read the following passages aloud. Read them clearly and express-ively whilst at the same time glancing at your audience.

(a) This passage:

The nature and purposes of lectures

THE Hale Committee's Report defines the lecture as 'a teach-ing period occupied wholly or mainly with *continuous exposi-tion by a lecturer.* Students attending it may be given some opportunity for questions or a little discussion, but in the main they have nothing to do except listen and take notes.'

The word 'lecture' itself, as I. A. Richards points out, is an unhappy one, because 'it suggests something designed to be read and read aloud, when most often any merit the thing might have would turn on its seeming to be given without notes and to be an exhibition of thinking, or, at least, of composition in progress. There are few matters concerning his craft which the teacher should study more than these differ-ences. They are its very elements. Speech and reading come to the ear and to the attention with different gaits. They are apt for different ends. They are vehicles which should have different cargoes. In spite of the many styles of each, what rides well in one commonly goes to bits in the other. It is odd, therefore, that so many teachers – and some eminent people are among them – will without compunction read out to their classes papers written for print – as though they had never been in an audience themselves. Odder still, how many, when they speak off the cuff, do their level best to sound like a slowed-down book. Talk of 'Teacher's Relation to the Student!' Nothing wrecks it more than these mismanagements.' (Quoted in Laing, 'The Art of Lecturing', in Layton (1968).

(b) A *brief* section from a text that you could quote in one of your lectures.

(c) This passage:
'Let me end this lecture on words and their history with this poem of Richard Church's, for it expresses more eloquently than I the themes of my lectures.

These Words

These daily words you listen to are not
One man's invention, but the growth of time,
Seeded from nobility and crime.
Some are blemished fruits, destined to rot
And fall. Some revive that were forgot.
A few, like death in life, may faintly chime
Dropped from the belfry of a poet's rhyme
Upon the graves in history's burial plot.
But all of them, long lived or quickly gone,
Are active powers, the radium of thought,
The close-packed atoms of our human story.
Here then is need for caution. Be admonished
To use these daily words as God-wrought
Magical master keys to right and glory.'

The lecture space

The first lectures probably took place under a tree with the students sitting literally and symbolically at the feet of their Greek masters. Later the Greeks built the Bouleuterion (c. 170 B.C.) for more formal gatherings. It was a semicircular amphitheatre.

In the Middle Ages lectures were readings or disputations between two lecturers or a lecturer and a student. They took place in the open air or in churches and halls. The lecturers stood in pulpits or on platforms, the students sat or stood on the floors. Sometimes they fought or quarrelled amongst themselves instead of listening to the rhetoric (Aries, 1973). Notes were not taken – scrolls and ink were precious. Instead, the good students attempted to listen, remember and understand; one suspects that the few who were successful had prodigious memories.

In Britain the first lecture theatre was built by Wren for the College of Physicians. In the nineteenth century the Royal Institution and some Oxford colleges acquired lecture theatres. The development of schools, mechanics' institutes, colleges and universities created interest in educational architecture. Goudet devised plans for lecture theatres for geology, chemistry and physics which took account of differences in demonstrations between these subjects. The chemistry theatres had a semicircular plan so that as many people as possible could see the objects and hear the speaker, whereas the physics theatres were rectangular since it was thought that full frontal presentation was all-important in physics.

Details of modern lecture theatres and the layout of equipment are described by Cannon and Kapelis (1976), Smith (1974) and Taylor (1974). Modern ones are often totally enclosed without windows and the seats are steeply raked and in long rows. They may contain a paraphernalia of devices such as electrically operated roller blackboards and screens, overhead projectors and television screens. There is a complex lighting system which, if you can work it, allows you to dim lights for showing slides or plunge the theatre into total darkness (the latter is easier to do than one expects). There is often a large demonstration bench and a lectern. Often the electrically operated blackboards and screens cannot be operated manually and the switches may be difficult to locate. Occasionally there is no chalk or overhead transparency pens. Lecture theatres can be hazardous places for the uninitiated.

Lecture rooms are smaller. They have windows which may enable you to see and hear traffic, lawn-mowers, aeroplanes, workmen, mechanical diggers and other students. The floor is horizontal so that people at the back cannot see you easily. There may be a platform, stage or dais which you can fall off. The blackboards are usually small, and sometimes an overhead projector and blackboard cannot be used simultaneously because the screen pulls down over the blackboard. Sometimes there are no curtains so that you cannot show slides. Electric sockets for equipment may be in unexpected places such as the back of the room – they are some-times more convenient for a student wishing to shave than a lecturer wanting to use equipment. The lecture room may contain desks, large benches or tables and enough chairs for the class. The entrance to the room may be close to where the lecturer stands, so that students who arrive late can unintentionally disrupt the lecture. Lecture rooms, like lecture theatres, contain hazards for the unsuspecting.

The spatial arrangements of lecture theatres and rooms, the furniture and fittings, all contribute to students perceiving the lecturer as an authority figure and expecting him to be such; they have symbolic as well as architectural meaning. In the lecture theatre, the lecturer is at the centre of the stage. He performs his task, he controls the lights as well as the knowledge he dispenses. The bench symbolises the barrier between the initiated, the lecturers, and the initiates, the students. The lecturer is at a distance from the students, physically and socially. He can more easily observe them than they can each other. Their attention is directed towards him.

Bennett and Bennett (1970) suggest that one can look at teaching spaces in terms of:

1 The container – its shape and size.
2 Props – furniture, fittings, costumes (such as gowns, customary dress).
3 Actors – the persons potentially involved in the interaction.
4 Modifiers – elements of light, sound, colour, temperature, humidity and the time of day. All of these affect concentration and reaction to teaching.
5 Duration – the time involved. A two-hour lecture is a very different experience from two one-hour lectures or four thirty-minute talks.
6 Progression – what the students experienced before and what they will be doing after the lecture or seminar. The last lecture of four in a morning is likely to be difficult for lecturers as well as students.

All of these have psychological as well as physiological effects on lectur-ing. A lecture given in a cubby-hole or shed on a hot summer's day is a different experience for everyone from a lecture given in a large air-conditioned theatre.

The most interesting set of studies on lecture space are reported by Sommer (1969), who deals with space, seating, territoriality and inter-action in lecture and seminar rooms, libraries, buses and residences. In one experiment he observed the seating choices and interactions of students in each of four rooms. One room was well-lit and ventilated, another was a storeroom without windows which had been converted into a lecture room, the third was a converted laundry room and the fourth a laboratory. The seats nearest the lecturer in three of these rooms were left empty since they were too close to him; latecomers sat in them if no other seat was available. In the fourth room, a long thin laboratory with high benches, the stools at the very back of the room were left empty. Most students usually chose the same seats or set of seats. In the lecture discussions those who sat in the front rows made more contributions than those in the middle rows, and those in the back rows contributed least. More contributions were made by people sitting in the middle of the rows than at the side. These results held for all four rooms.

Guyot (1970) found a close relationship between habitual choice of seats and the students' attitudes towards the lecturer and other students. The relationships were complex but, roughly speaking, those with the most favourable attitudes to the lecturer and to other students sat towards the middle of the rooms, those who were coolly disposed to the lecturer and other students sat in the corners at the back.

Sommer's experiments demonstrate some of the effects of space and seating upon interaction, Guyot's the relationship between seating and attitudes. Singer (1964) in one modest but interesting survey of 192 women students looked at seating, interaction patterns and personality in relation to levels of achievement. In more homely terms, he investigated who were the high achievers, where they sat and what they did that was different from low achievers. He found that attractive first-born girls obtained significantly more high-grade point averages. These tended to sit near the front of the lecture class, to listen more attentively, to talk to the lecturers more frequently afterwards and to make more appointments with them. Miller and Parlett's (1974) study of the examination game also noted that many high achievers talked more frequently to lecturers after lectures and made more appointments.

ACTIVITY 27 – Checking a lecture room

Visit one of the lecture rooms (or theatres) that you use. Check the position of plugs, screens, blackboard and the view of these from different parts of the room. Draw a rough sketch of the room and make a few notes on its good and bad points and suggest ways in which it could be improved. Meet in a small group and report on the rooms that you have investigated. Decide whether you propose to take any action to improve the facilities. If so, what action do you propose?

Summary

This Unit has introduced you to some ideas, findings and procedures which are relevant, if not essential, to the task of lecturing. It began with a discussion of anxieties about lecturing, which was followed by a simple model of how students learn from lectures and some basic skills of lecturing. The final section moved out into space – the lecture space. Throughout the Unit there were activities designed to help you pool experiences with colleagues, to share problems and to sharpen up various essential skills of lecturing.

Unit Four – Learning about the structure of lectures

The previous Unit dealt with several aspects of lecturing. This deals with only one: the structure of lectures. Having read it and carried out the activities, you should be able to identify various lecture methods and to state their strengths and weaknesses, and you will have had some practice in miniaturised versions of the more complex ones.

Contrary to popular opinion, there is not just one way of structuring a lecture but several. Fortunately Donald Bligh (1972) has provided a useful system of classification, and this Unit draws heavily on his observations and suggestions as well as on observations of lectures given in various faculties of the University of Nottingham. Although we thus have a framework for classifying lectures, it is not, however, suggested that every lecture fits snugly into the classification system – some contain elements of all the methods outlined below.

A lecture is a set of key points with associated examples, illustrations, elaborations and qualifications. The set of keys may be ordered in several ways, and each order represents a different lecture method. Just as the order of keys in music can provide variations upon a theme, so the order of keys of a lecture can offer varying emphases on information, understanding and interest. And just as we can identify various structural forms in music, so we can identify structures of lectures. The rich diversity of lectures may be classified into five main types: the classical, the problem-centred, the sequential, the comparative and the thesis. These are ideal types, or stripped-down versions of reality. They reveal the underlying structures and purposes and, in so doing, suggest strategies for maximising their effectiveness and minimising confusion.

PHYSICAL AND BIOLOGICAL METHODS OF DISEASE PREVENTION IN FRUIT

INTRODUCTION

Physical and biological
methods of prevention > Chemical prevention > Cure (eradication)

     better than   better than

MAJOR POINTS

(i) *Site of new plantation*

– Climate < rainfall
            temperature

– Site (altitude and topography) < Wind
                                   Frosts

                                   Radiation – frosts

– Soil < Soil characteristics
         Soil cropping history

   General   Specific replant

(ii) *Planting healthy material*
   – Nuclear stock association (approach)

(iii) *Planting resistant varieties*
   – Role in strawberry production (example of failure)

SUMMARY

Fig. 4   Example of the classical method

The classical method

In the classical method the lecture is divided into broad sections, these sections into separate sub-sections and, perhaps, again into still smaller units. Each sub-section may be a key, i.e. contain a key point and perhaps examples, qualifications and a brief summary. Fig. 4 shows the structure of a lecture on horticulture based on the classical method. It was prepared in that form by a young lecturer on a course for newly appointed lecturers. It shows clearly his proposed structure, and his main themes are readily understood. Not all topics may be so comprehensible to non-specialists but setting out the structure of a lecture in this way is likely to improve its intelligibility to you as well as to your students.

The classical method is by far the most common form of lecture. It appears easy to plan, is probably the easiest to takes notes from and is particularly useful for outlining the main features of a topic such as 'The principal effects of cholesterol', 'The distribution network of the Central Electricity Generating Board', or 'Some themes of metaphysical poetry'. The structure of the classical method is more readily discernible in lectures on science than in those on literary subjects. Yet if one can penetrate the eloquent phrases and sparkling metaphors of many lectures upon literature, the classical method is often there, underpinning the jewels of wisdom or the pastiche.

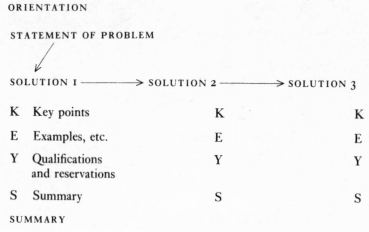

Fig. 5   Lecturing – the problem-centred method

To make good use of the classical method is not as easy as it may appear. First, you have to have a clear grasp of what you propose to tackle – and ignore – in the lecture. Second, you need to classify each main section clearly. Third, when lecturing you need to indicate clearly when you are beginning and ending each section. This may be done by a blackboard summary or by verbal markers such as 'So [pause] the main point is. . . . Now let's turn to the next subsection of this section on. . . .' Without these simple signposts, what began as the classical method of lecturing becomes a mish-mash.

The method has one other major pitfall for the unwary. Because it is relatively easy to catalogue and recite fact after fact, it is easy to grind on relentlessly and generate bordeom rather than understanding. Thus one needs to use apt examples and illustrations in an interesting, lively way. This requires thought, planning and attention to detail in presentation.

Before reading on, you might like to try sketching an example of the classical method in your own subject.

How are language and thinking related?

Introduction: Basic problems are: Do we think in words? Is what we say thoughts as well as words? Do we store information in words? May be summarised as: Do we think as we speak? Do we speak as we think?

1   Possibilities. Tackle each in turn.
Language and thought not related at all.
Probably true in very early stage of development.
Not true. Experimental and anecdotal evidence. Vygotsky, etc.

2   Language and thinking identical. (Speak in words, think in words.) Some evidence we speak silently when thinking (e.g. Jacobson, etc.). *But* depends on definition of language and thinking. What counts as thinking and not thinking – dreams, reasoning, etc. What counts as language and not language – symbolic communication, etc.
Language and thought not identical.

3   Language and thinking overlap.
Some thinking is internalised symbolic communication.
Some language usage is not product of thinking – but learnt habit.
Overlap looks something like this. Show chart.

Fig. 6   Example of problem–centred method

The problem-centred method

This is useful for examining alternative views and solutions to such problems as 'What is the relationship between body and mind', 'How are language and thought interrelated?', 'Was Forster a great novelist?'

All problem-centred lectures contain a statement of a problem, explicit or implicit criteria statements and evaluative ones. For my part I prefer explicit criteria statements, since they reduce confusion and ambiguity, but not all lecturers agree. The statements may be presented in the form of keys as in fig. 5, which depicts the main structure of the method. Fig. 6 shows an example produced by a lecturer in psychology. Again you will note that the structure of the lecture enables you to understand what the lecturer was trying to explain although you may not be conversant with the field.

A necessary but not sufficient condition of success with this method is a clear, brief statement of the problem. Without this the structure of the lecture crumbles. The method also requires the selection of the main alternative solutions and clear statements of the main points or evidence in favour of each solution followed by an equally clear statement against it. The approach can be intellectually stimulating, particularly if it is combined with expressed enthusiasm for the problem and the use of rhetorical devices such as: 'So, Pasteur demonstrated to his own satisfaction that.... Now [pause] some of you may think he was right. But was he? Let's look now at what Koch had to say....'

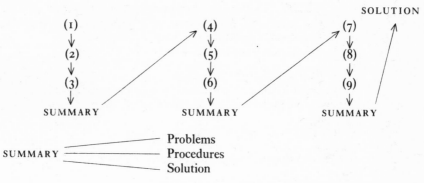

ORIENTATION

STATEMENT OF PROBLEM

KEYS

SOLUTION

(1)
(2)
(3)
SUMMARY

(4)
(5)
(6)
SUMMARY

(7)
(8)
(9)
SUMMARY

SUMMARY ——————— Problems
——————— Procedures
——————— Solution

Fig. 7   Lecturing – the sequential method

The problem-centred method is not only intellectually stimulating, it is also, alas, easy to fudge. Common errors are unclear, excessively long statements of the problem, confused statements for and against solutions, the introduction of asides and the frequent impulsive cross-referencing of alternative solutions. Stick to the main lines of enquiry if you use this method and be sure to summarise at the end of each alternative solution and again at the end of the lecture. The most appropriate point for cross-referencing alternative solutions is in the final summary. At that point you can also ask a question for the students to think about in their own time, such as 'Now, the really interesting question is: were Pasteur's methods, after all, the best ones? The decision [pause] is yours.'

Before reading on you might like to try sketching an example of the problem-centred method from your own subject.

The sequential method

The sequential method consists of a series of linked statements which

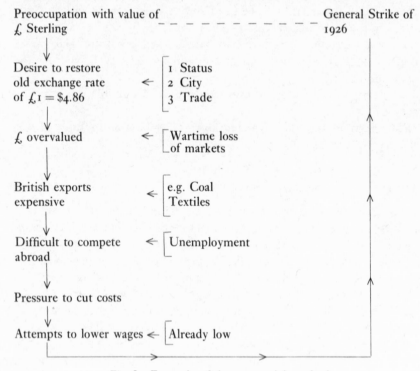

Why did preoccupation with the value of sterling lead to the general strike?

Fig. 8   Example of the sequential method

lead, usually, to a conclusion. It is used in historical accounts, and these can occur in the sciences as well as in history and other arts subjects. It is employed in literature to describe the main themes of a work and in philosophy to argue a logical case. In all of these it is important to highlight the main points. A history lecturer who merely recites facts and dates in order without indicating their importance is likely to be neither interesting nor illuminating.

The method is the most common, however, in mathematics-based subjects. Here it *looks* easy. You simply fill the blackboard with symbols and talk to them, not to the students. In fact, it is the most difficult method to make meaningful and interesting, and it is the easiest to fudge. One has to ensure that the steps are within the grasp of the students and to summarise frequently the main steps and procedures. Triple integration in the head may be easy for lecturers in mathematics and physics but not for most other people. To make it interesting, you can show the relevance of the proofs to other topics and problems, indicate their historical origins, their applications and perhaps their beauty. To avoid confusions you have to be sure that the summaries on the blackboard or overhead transparency can be clearly seen. Most important of all, if you make a mistake, apologise, accept the groans, point out that it is better to have a valid proof and start again – don't simply draw arrows and inserts and mutter, 'Well, you get the general idea'.

Fig. 7 sets out the basic structure and fig. 8 an example produced by a lecturer.

Before reading on, you might like to try sketching an example of this method in your own subject.

ACTIVITY 28 – Search for structure

Look through some notes you took as an undergraduate or some lecture notes. Select an example of a lecture predominantly using the classical, the problem-centred or the sequential method. Prepare a summary of it which is suitable for display on a small blackboard or by overhead projector. Describe the main structure of the lecture in no more than five minutes to the other members of the group, who should discuss briefly (no more than five minutes) the structure, the content and the difficulties they and students might have in understanding and taking notes from it. If possible, members of the group should between them present all three methods of lecturing.

This activity should help you to become aware of the different lecture methods, to revise some of your content and to use your skills in explaining. It is a particularly interesting and challenging exercise when the group includes members from several disciplines.

Other types of lecture method

The classical, problem-centred and sequential methods of lecturing are the main types. Obviously not all lectures closely approximate to them, and many contain features of all three. In addition there are two others, the comparative method and the thesis, which contain elements of the major types.

THE COMPARATIVE METHOD

This is, as its name implies, a comparison of two or more processes, themes, works, theories, ideas or systems. It may be a search for similarities or differences, for advantages or disadvantages. At its most complex it deals with the former, and is analogous to the familiar examination question 'Compare and Contrast'. Figs. 9 and 10 set out a possible structure and an example.

The comparative method has elements in common with the classical and sequential ones. It may use division into major sections which contain sub-sections dealing with similarities and differences. Alternatively, all the similarities may be dealt with together in a main section and then the crucial differences considered. The explanation of the differences and, more rarely, of the similarities may require a sequence of reasoning. Occasionally they may be presented as problems, in which case all three methods are in use.

Orientation   X *versus* Y

Characteristics

I
2
3
4
5

Summary

Fig. 9   Lecturing – the comparative method

MARX AND WEBER'S VIEWS ON SOCIAL CLASS

ORIENTATION   Both important. Both *appear* to have similar views but there are important differences. Hence this lecture. It will be oversimplified. See references.

MARX   Crudely, class system is exploitative. Class defined primarily in economic terms. Based upon modes of production, etc.

WEBER   Class is multidimensional. Distinguishes class, status and power. Shows interrelationships.

MARX AND WEBER COMPARED ON
Economic determinism, definitions of class, relationship of class with other concepts. Usefulness for analysing modern industrial society. Table of conclusions.

SUMMARY OF SIMILARITIES

SUMMARY OF DIFFERENCES

Fig. 10   Example of the comparative method

The comparative method is intellectually demanding for lecturers as well as students, and also puts a heavy load on students' short-term memories. It is easy to confuse – and become confused – in this method. Building up a summary on the blackboard or overhead transparency as one lectures reduces this and keeps one on course. In the introduction it is advisable, as usual, to spell out clearly what you propose to do and to indicate briefly the criteria or themes of the comparison. The method is particularly useful for showing students how to tackle comparative problems. It is also useful for drawing together and comparing different approaches or theories which may have been presented and studied during a course. Try sketching an example of this method in your own subject before reading on.

THE THESIS METHOD

This method begins with an assertion and proceeds to justify it by bringing together a wide range of evidence and argument which may be presented in major sections or in problem form. It may include theses and countertheses. At one lecture I attended, the lecturer began with the remark: 'Today I am going to prove to you that Queen Elizabeth the First was a bastard – er – technically speaking of course.' He went on to describe the married life of Ann Boleyn, pointed to the usual conclusion drawn by textbooks on the Elizabethan Period, questioned their

ORIENTATION

Statement of main thesis. Main implications or deductions. Description of method used to tackle thesis.

RESTATEMENT OF THESIS

1 First implication → Evidence and assumptions → Conclusion
2 ..   ..
3 ..   ..
4 ..   ..

SUMMARY AND CONCLUSION

NOTE: Each implication may be divided into subsections. 1–4 may be a sequence of reasons or merely a set of related information. The thesis may be 'proved', 'disproved' or stated as 'not proven'.

Fig. 11   The thesis method

MASIA'S THEORY OF THE RULING CLASS (1896)

1 ORIENTATION

Masia's basic theory
1 All societies have a ruling class.
2 It is small in size.
3 It has a political ideology which unites it.
4 It relies upon the second stratum for opinion, leaders, civil servants, for recruitment and to alert leaders to dissatisfactions.

2 Propose to tackle each of these in turn by looking at empirical evidence and his argument.

1
2
3
4

3 SUMMARY

Conditions 1 and 2 appear to hold (generally). 3 and 4 hold under conditions of stability.

Fig. 12   First example of the thesis method

validity and then proceeded to cite lesser-known evidence, from which he drew conclusions. He then coupled these conclusions with doubts about various historians' conclusions and ended with the suggestion that Queen Elizabeth I was probably illegitimate.

Figs. 11 and 12 set out a structure and an example of the method; fig. 13 is an example based on a four-minute explanation. Like the comparative method the thesis is intellectually challenging. It requires careful preparation and skilful delivery, otherwise the thesis and the audience may be lost. Try sketching an example of this method from your own subject.

ORIENTATION

Going to prove that an absolute democracy cannot exist in a society that wants to maintain individual preferences. To do this, will use axiomatic choice theory.

1 Describe axiomatic choice theory – transitivity, comparability.

2 Model of two-person economy (Adam and Eve)
  Adam $X > Y > Z$ Eve $Y > X > Z$
  Show contradiction

3 CONCLUSION

Fig. 13   Second example of the thesis method

ACTIVITY 29 – Explaining a comparison or thesis

Prepare a four-minute explanation of a small topic within your subject using the comparative or the thesis method. Give the explanation to members of your group, following the instructions in Activity 2. View and discuss the explanations. Use the Guidelines for explaining revisited (p. 35) as a focus for discussion.

ACTIVITY 30 – A thesis explanation

Below is a tapescript of an explanation using the thesis method. The lecturer presented his argument on an overhead projector as well as orally. The structure is given in fig. 11 and you might enjoy analysing it. Could you improve on it? How?

A tapescript of a thesis explanation

ORIENTATION

Right. I'm going to explain or hope to demonstrate that an absolute democracy in a sense of individuals' preferences, society being composed in sum of individuals, an absolute democracy can never exist, if it wants to maintain individual preferences.

It is done by a thing called axiomatic choice theory and what that means is that we have axioms or assumptions about the way people behave and the choice bit is that people have preferences, that people make choices in society.

INTERPRETATIVE

Let's set up the axiom system first.

Axiom one, up here [points to overhead projection] is called the transitivity axiom. And this one says that if we have three states of the world X, Y, and Z, these are states – what people want, what people prefer, anything, just states of the world. Z is preferred to Y, Y is preferred to X, Z would be preferred to X. Simple example, 8's bigger than 4 which is bigger than 2 – so 8's bigger than 2.

The next axiom [points at projection] the comparability axiom is if X is preferred to Y and also within that society Y is preferred to X we say we – society cannot make a judgement, society cannot actively prefer, therefore it must be indifferent between those states of the world, in this case X and Y, it must be indifferent. In this case it prefers, the sign for prefer [writes on projector] – in this case indifferent.

REASON–GIVING

Let's use a simple example, a two-person economy. Adam and Eve. Now, Adam, it so happened on historical record preferred X to Y to Z whereas Eve, being feminine, preferred Y to Z to X, the same symbolic notion as we had up here [points to projector].

Now, as our two individuals we want to generate an absolutely democratic society so their preferences, their individual preferences are going to be represented in society, we hope. Let's add 'em up, because society is just Adam plus Eve, – well, in the first stages anyway.

Adam we see prefers X to Y, Eve prefers Y to X – from our second axiom society is indifferent between Y and X – from axiom two.

Looking at these again we see that Adam prefers Y to Z, Eve prefers Y to Z – hallelujah! Everybody prefers Y to Z. And from combining these two society also prefers Y to Z.

Y equals X, Y is greater than Z, therefore X is greater than Z.

Next stage of the argument from there – Adam prefers X to Z but Eve prefers Z to X. Society is therefore indifferent between X and Z. But if we stand back and look at it we've got a horrible mess, because this means that society is indifferent between X, Y and Z. But it also preferred X to Z. It just won't work. It's impossible. And that is why it is called the impossibility theorem.

CONCLUSION

So, what I'm saying, in a sense, is that if you want a democratic situation in which individuals' views are represented within society you cannot get it unless everyone has the same preference ordering. If everyone preferred X to Y to Z – great – because the society would prefer X to Y to Z. We have the very strange situation that your absolutely democratic society is therefore totalitarian. Think about it.

Thank you.

Summary

This Unit has been concerned with the structure of various lecture methods and their strengths and weaknesses. A lecture is a set of key points with associated illustrations, examples, elaborations and qualifications. The set of keys may be ordered in several ways, and each order represents a lecture method. Five major structures were identified: the classical, problem-centred, sequential, comparative and thesis methods. Not all lectures are pure examples of them. The activities were designed to increase your awareness of the structure of lectures and to give you some practice in miniaturised versions of the more complex forms of lecture method.

Unit Five – Learning to lecture

The technique of imparting knowledge in the special way called lecturing can be learned and improved upon.   (Pear, 1933, p. 145)

This Unit is concerned with the task of lecturing. It is divided into four sections: the first deals with the preparation of lecture materials; the second provides hints and suggestions on giving lectures; the third outlines various ways of observing and analysing them; and the fourth section discusses briefly how to plan a series of lectures. Having read this Unit and carried out the activities, you should be able to prepare lectures, give them, evaluate them and plan lecture courses. Many of you will already have had some experience of these tasks, but it is hoped that this Unit together with the previous ones will enable you to tackle them more efficiently and effectively. All the sections of this Unit contain hints and suggestions which are offered as guidelines, not as rigid prescriptions. Nonetheless, perhaps you will try all of them before deciding whether to accept, modify or reject.

Before reading the Unit, you should try the next activity, which is time-consuming and difficult. You need to follow the instructions carefully if you are to gain the maximum benefit.

ACTIVITY 31 – Explaining a lecture

1   Select a topic which you think students will find interesting from an early part of a lecture course you are planning and prepare a lecture on it (usually 55 or 60 minutes). You may, if you wish, use the first lecture you intend actually to give. When you have prepared it, draw up a brief itemised summary of its

key points in a form suitable for a small blackboard or overhead transparency.

2 Prepare and give a brief, simplified, five-minute explanation of the content and structure of your lecture to the group of peers you are working with. This should include reasons for the structure you have chosen for the lecture. Use the itemised summary as a focus for your explanation. State clearly how you will introduce the lecture, the main keys, the links between the keys and the summary. Indicate the sections of the lecture you think may be difficult for you to present to the students, or for them to understand. The other members of the group should take notes of your talk using the guidelines given in paragraph 4 below. The five-minute explanations may be video-recorded if you wish, but it is better to spend more time discussing the structure of the lecture than video-recording and viewing. If all the five-minute explanations are video-recorded, take a break, then view and discuss each recording in turn.

3 The discussion should centre round the following questions:
   (a) What were the central questions of your lecture? What did you expect students to learn or understand from your lecture?
   (b) What type of lecture methods did you use?
   (c) Was the orientation clear and interesting?
   (d) Were the sections of the lecture clearly organised and clearly linked?
   (e) Were the main keys clear and accurate and linked?
   (f) Were your examples and illustrations apt?
   (g) Were any reservations and qualifications you made clear and brief?
   (h) Were your brief summaries and *final summary* clear and coherent?
   (i) What activities, if any, will students have to carry out in your lecture?
   (j) What possible weaknesses are there likely to be in your presentation? What steps do you propose to combat them?
   (k) Are the group of students you are lecturing to likely to understand your lecture? How do you intend to discover this?

4 Members of the group should listen carefully to the explanations of each other's lectures, try to answer the above questions and offer suggestions, if necessary, for improving the content and

structure. Whilst listening to the explanations they should take notes along the following guidelines. These notes should be used in the discussion.

(a) What was the central question(s) with which the lecture was concerned?

(b) What were the major keys? Were they clear in themselves? How were the major keys related?

(c) Did the lecture appear to be predominantly classical, problem–centred, sequential, comparative, thesis or 'other'?

Preparing and designing lectures

Activity 31 gave you an opportunity to prepare a lecture and discuss it with colleagues, and required you to apply the principles of explaining to a complex task. The activity showed you how others tackle the preparation of lectures and it may have reminded you that listening and note-taking are not easy.

You will also have realised that this section on preparing and designing lectures comes after you have actually tried to do this. This is because most people, when given several hints and suggestions before they tackle lecture preparation, get confused; after an attempt, hints and suggestions become more meaningful. Some of them have already been discovered during the activity, some come from other participants, and a few may be new.

However, a few errors are often made in Activity 31. Some lecturers merely recite a list of topics without indicating how they are related. The instructions for the activity ask for 'central questions' and 'links', but these instructions are frequently ignored. Some lecturers do not consider precisely what they are trying to explain in their lectures or what they expect their students to learn.

This section provides hints, suggestions and a set of steps to help you prepare lectures more efficiently and, thus, with less risk of errors.

STRUCTURE AND PRESENTATION

Unit One on explaining emphasised that structure and presentation have to be seen by explainees as clear and interesting. It also stressed that the orientation and summary are particularly important, as well as apt examples and clear links between sections of an explanation.

All this applies with even more force to lecturing. The orientation, pattern of keys and summary are the foundations of lecture preparation and design. But here, there is a serious difficulty for those seeking evidence about the best pattern for major keys. As yet we do not know enough about lectures and lecturing in various subjects, and one cannot prescribe rigid patterns of keys for another lecturer even if one knows the topic and his students intimately. However, one can offer suggestions which are based on experimental evidence from studies of lectures and classrooms.

Firstly, one should use examples and illustrations to reveal the underlying principles. Whether the examples should follow or precede the principles is not clear. My suspicion is that lectures which proceed from examples to principles are more comprehensible and more interesting than those which state formal principles at length with few or no examples – this appears to be true from the Nottingham studies of explaining (see p. 11).

Secondly, one should outline features rather than cram in fine detail. Erskine and O'Morchoe (1961) showed this in their experiment on teaching anatomy and it does not appear to have been contradicted in the teaching of other subjects. Too much detail can produce mental dazzle (Katz, 1956). The detail can be culled from books once the essential features have been recognised and understood.

Thirdly, *very* highly structured presentations are likely to be nonproductive because they are extremely difficult to follow orally.

These hints are useful but they do not tell us the best way of patterning keys, only the better ways. Until they are disproved, the pedagogical maxims of Herbart (1893) – proceed from the known to the unknown, the concrete to the abstract and the simple to the complex – should be taken as a guide, but not as a rigid law.

WHERE TO START

At this stage you may be nodding your head and saying: 'Yes, I know that structure and presentation are important. What worries me is how do I decide what to lecture on, what to read and how much.' I have some suggestions on these matters which, unless you are a psychologist, may seem strange.

Write down the topic of your lecture in the centre of a blank piece of paper, then write down whatever comes into your head about it, no matter how trivial or nonsensical it seems. Gradually you will find ideas and questions coming to you from all sorts of areas. Write similar ideas and questions close to each other. Start different sets of them on different parts of the sheet. Do this for about five minutes and you will probably have the embryo of a lecture. The method works in all subjects, including mathematics and physics. Indeed, mathematicians are sometimes surprised at the connections and links they discover for themselves in their own subject. The method is known as 'free association'.

Then begin reading. Choose only a few texts or articles and gut them. Note the authors' headings and subheadings as well as the content and jot down any further ideas and questions on the free association sheet. Do not read too many texts and articles at this stage or you will become confused and confusing. Remember that you are searching for essential features and principles and not for fine detail.

Then draw up a rough plan of the order of the lecture, bearing in mind that you want the students to understand and be interested in it. This is best done by posing simple questions beginning with 'what?', 'how?' and 'why?' Some more details are given after the next activity, which is for small groups. Do try it first.

ACTIVITY 32 – Associating with psychologists

Imagine you have been appointed to a temporary lectureship in a department of psychology. The professor meets you in a corridor and asks you what you are doing next Tuesday afternoon. You reply, 'Nothing'. 'Good', he says, 'Could you take my first-year lecture on perception. There are only about 200 students and most of them are doing psychology as a subsidiary.' You ask him which aspects of perception and he shrugs his shoulders and says 'Anything you like' as he walks away....

Now take a blank piece of paper, write 'perception' in the middle of it, then say and scribble whatever comes into your heads about it. One person should be the official scribe, but everyone should say and scribble on their own sheets. Do this for a couple of minutes and then, as a group, try to work out the proposed structure of the lecture. If more than one group are doing the activity, compare the structure and content of the proposed lectures. The activity should take no more than fifteen minutes. A similar one on 'measurement' or 'imagery' may be used but 'perception' is more interesting to groups drawn from several disciplines and their approaches are often very different.

The steps of preparing and designing lectures

Here are a set of steps which experienced and less experienced lecturers may like to try when preparing a few lectures. One try is not enough to get the feel of the approach.

Step 1 – What do I want the students to learn?

The first step is, obviously, to decide or discover what you are going to lecture on. What are the students going to learn from your lecture? At this stage you may only have a topic in mind, such as alkaloids, Donne's poetry or cost effectiveness. So you need to frame questions which focus more sharply on what you intend to deal with, e.g. 'What are the main types of alkaloid?', 'What are the underlying themes of Donne's poetry?', 'How does Donne use imagery and symbol?', 'How may cost effectiveness be measured?' Such questions give a focus to your lecture and help you to define the boundaries of what you will or will not discuss in it.

Step 2 – Free association

Most of you will not be lecturing on your special topic. Some of you may have topics which you did not study as undergraduates, and all of you will want to prepare your lectures efficiently, without undue waste of time. One way of simplifying your task is to use free association – even if you are not familiar with the topic (see Activity 32). Write down your question in the middle of a blank page and then jot down any ideas, facts or questions which occur to you. Try to group them as you go along, then cross out those which are irrelevant or barely relevant and ring those areas which seem important.

Step 3 – Read

Step 2 may have seemed strange. Yet if you tried it (as I hope you did!) you will have discovered you do have the embryonic beginnings of a lecture. You also have a focus for your reading and note-taking. Read only the relevant sections from a few texts or articles and note the headings and their structure, as well as the relevant content. As you read and take notes, also jot down any key questions or important areas you may have missed on the free association page.

Step 4 – Organise

Now look at the question you framed. Decide if it is the right one. If not, recast it and, if necessary, free associate and read a little more. If it is the right question, set out a rough summary of your lecture. This can also serve as a rough draft of any handout you may wish to give.

Step 5 – Set the lecture out
Write out the lecture in note form, so that you will speak to the audience rather than read to them. Have a generous margin for additional notes, leave space between major sections and use clear headings. Summarise the main points of the lecture on one sheet (examples were given in figs. 6–15). Indicate the orientation, the main sections and their key points, examples, etc., any qualifications and restatements, and the final summary. Pay particular attention to the orientation and summary and links between keys and sections.

A major difficulty in lecturing is holding the attention of the audience. I have already mentioned the importance of preparing interesting examples and of the use of non-verbal cues in giving explanations. You might also, at this stage, build into your lecture some simple activities, such as an easy problem to solve or a question to be discussed by small groups (sections of rows of the audience), or tape or film. A few interesting asides and anecdotes also help, provided that the former are clearly asides and that the latter are funny and, preferably, apt. Finally, note down on a sheet any equipment, slides, transparencies, tapes, etc., you will need. Place this on the top of your lecture notes with the lecture summary.

(Step 6 – Rehearse it if it's your first lecture)
A difficulty most of us have in lecturing is timing. If you are very conscientious you might audio-record a rehearsal of your lecture. About 35 minutes of continuous audio-recording is equivalent to 50 minutes in the lecture theatre.

ACTIVITY 33 – Lecturing revisited

Read through the notes, comments and suggestions made on the lecture you prepared in Activity 31, and restructure the lecture. Then prepare another one. This time follow the steps of lecture preparation and design carefully. When you have done this, draw up a summary suitable for showing on an overhead transparency or a small blackboard during a five-minute explanation, and discuss it with the members of the group (see Activity 31, for further details). How has your knowledge of approaches to lecture preparation and design changed since Activity 31?

Giving lectures

From the moment you enter the lecture room you are creating impressions and being assessed by the students. Hence the importance of the first lecture and, in this book, of the various activities on explaining, on methods, skills and styles, and on the preparation and design of lectures. Unfortunately a lecture can be well prepared and look elegant on paper but be ruined by mundane errors in performance. Simple actions can make it clear and stimulating – one has to take steps to ensure that the actual delivery is good. The activities on explaining were much concerned with these (rather than repeat them here, see pages 30–4). Look at the hints and guidelines just before you give your first lecture, check the lecture room, the materials and equipment, and read through your lecture notes and insert any last-minute inspirations.

Whilst giving the lecture look at various students in all parts of the audience: although they are not talking, their non-verbal cues may tell you things.

If someone asks a question unexpectedly and you cannot answer it immediately, say so. If you will be answering it later in the lecture, tell them that rather than answer it there and then. Confident, non-aggressive, responses to such questions are usually best – if only because aggression may be perceived as insecurity.

A difficulty most of us have is timing. If your lecture is too short, then stop; don't flannel. If your lecture is too long, don't run over time. Stop a minute or so before the end of the lecture period, summarise the lecture so far and say that you will continue on the next occasion. You should find that after a term you get the timing right – usually.

Soon after giving the lecture, spend a few minutes modifying the organisation of its content and presentation. Look again at the hints on explaining (p. 35) and jot down notes of errors and, more important, ways of improving the lecture. Insert any examples or analogies which you used spontaneously and successfully, delete any parts which now seem irrelevant, and modify any which seemed unclear or particularly boring.

Not all the lectures in a course can be made stimulating – sometimes one has to tackle important topics which do not come alive easily. If the topic is important but you cannot make it more interesting, say that it is important and why; warn the students that it may be difficult to follow. If it is relatively unimportant and uninteresting, don't lecture on it but, instead, give a good specific reference or a handout, or organise a different learning experience. Nonetheless, in any course of twelve lectures you should aim to give at least three which are stimulating, one at the beginning, one in the middle and one towards the end.

If you can, provide brief lecture summaries. One sheet should be sufficient per lecture, and it should contain the key points, important bibliographical references used, and precise suggestions for further reading. The handouts may be given out just before the lecture, and can be referred to in the orientation and again in the summary. They need not contain the answers to the questions you are posing if this will spoil your presentation. If you are using a problem-centred approach it may be best to give out the brief summary sheet at the end of the lecture.

Observing and analysing lectures

Observation and analysis are the bases of evaluation. This section will show you a few methods of observing and analysing lectures which you may use to evaluate your own.

At the outset, a distinction needs to be made between observing and analysing the processes and the products of lecturing. Processes are the activities and reactions of lecturers and students that may be observed directly in lectures or in recordings of them. Products are the outcomes, which may either be from students or lecturers. They may be students' later reactions to a lecture, their recall or understanding of it, the attitude changes resulting from it, the lecturer's own reactions to his lecture and what he may have learnt about a topic from the act of lecturing on it.

The processes of lecturing may be observed and analysed by students, other lecturers or observers; recordings of a lecture may be analysed by the lecturer himself. Methods of observing lectures range from impression gathering to complex analytical methods which require trained observers. There is no text or article which sets out their diversity although Tribe and Gibbs (1977) and Elton (1977, personal communication) are developing some systems for analysing lectures and S.A.I.D. (Brown and Armstrong, 1977) is being used to analyse tapescripts of them.

Product studies of lectures have been with us since the examination system began. But examination results measure students' knowledge, abilities, aptitudes and maturation as well as the quality of a lecture course; their characteristics and performance do not entirely depend on a lecturer's prowess. Nonetheless, consistently poor or outstanding results in examinations do provide useful indications of the quality of a lecture course. Product studies involving lecturers' reactions and learning from their own lecturing have not, as far as I know, received much attention.

84 Unit Five

Despite the absence of research on the processes and products of lecturing, there are several simple methods which lecturers may use to evaluate their lectures and to increase their sensitivity to students' feedback signals. A selection of these methods is given below, and it begins with some activities on the latter. Carry out Activity 34 before reading on.

GATHERING IMPRESSIONS

ACTIVITY 34 – Recalling impressions

(a) Imagine you are in a lecture room. The lecturer is mumbling and occasionally he writes an indecipherable sentence on the blackboard. The students are bored and listless. Close your eyes, try to picture them, how they are sitting, their body positions and their facial expressions. How do they look? Jot down brief descriptions of various individuals.

(b) Now imagine you are in a lecture room where the lecturer is talking animatedly and pointing to words and a diagram on the board. The audience are very interested. Close your eyes, try to picture them, how they are sitting, their body positions and their facial expressions. Jot down brief descriptions of various individuals.

If you do this activity in a group, compare your notes and compile a list of feedback signals.

In your jottings you may have noted that some bored students are slouching, or are turned slightly away from the lecturer. They may rest their heads on their hands and they often try to hide their faces, which may be expressionless. Their eyelids may be partially closed and their mouths turned down. A few students may be doodling, or knitting, or writing letters. Occasionally, in a very bored group, a student will involuntarily drop his head. He's had enough.

Interested audiences usually sit with their heads slightly forward and their eyes wide open. They look towards the lecturer. Some of them will exchange glances of approval – for the lecturer, not each other – and some will be smiling and nodding agreement. A few will lean forward, draw in breath and open their mouths as if they want to speak.

This brief description does not cover all the possible signals of interest or boredom but it should be sufficient to give you the 'feel' of bored and interested individuals in lectures and seminars. Time-lapse photography of lecture audiences will, no doubt, increase our knowledge of these signals. As yet, no such studies have been reported although there have been a few of attending behaviours in pupils (MacGraw, 1965; Fanslow, 1965; Grobe and Pettibone, 1973). In the meantime you might like to try the following activities which are designed to sharpen your perception of students' reactions during lectures. Perception is an integral part of the lecture process, since you can modify your lecture to match the perceived needs and reactions of the students – if you wish to.

ACTIVITY 35 – Gathering impressions

Ask a colleague if you can sit in on one of his lectures in order to observe the students. Choose a place in the lecture room where you can see most of them and you are not disturbing the lecturer.

Select six students to observe: two who are sitting close to the front, two in the middle and one in each of the back corners of the class. If possible, choose three men and three women. Observe each student in turn for one minute and repeat this sequence throughout the lecture. A one-hour lecture will thus give you ten one-minute observations of each of the six students. Use the sign system shown below for recording observations. Soon after the lecture analyse the data you have collected and prepare a brief report. Discuss the reports with other colleagues who have carried out the activity, and also what you have learnt from it.

Student reactions in lectures
Set out the following sign system on squared paper. Tick any reaction when it occurs for the first time within the minute observations, i.e. do not tick the same thing more than once per minute.
Listening
Looking at lecturer
Looking at blackboard
Writing
Smiling
Nodding agreement
Looking interested
Playing with pens, etc.
Talking to neighbours
Looking round the room
Day-dreaming

Writing continuously without
    attending to lecturer
Looking bored
Looking restless

ACTIVITY 36 – Recounted impressions

Ask a colleague to carry out Activity 35 on one of your lectures. He
or she should write a report and show you the original data. Discuss the report and your general impressions of students' reactions
during the lecture.

USING STUDENTS' REACTIONS TO LECTURES

It is probably easier to fool one's colleagues and oneself about teaching
prowess than it is to fool one's students. As Aristotle is reputed to have
said, 'You get a better notion of the merits of the dinner from the dinner
guests than you do from the cook' (quoted by Flood-Page, 1974).

Students' reactions to a lecture or lecture course may be gathered
casually in conversation or obtained systematically through rating schedules and written reports. Rating schedules which contain a section for
comments are probably better than either just rating schedules or discussions on their own: discussions may be dominated by vociferous critics,
and rating schedules contain only the items that you think are important.
Written reports may not cover all aspects of a lecture and are difficult to
analyse. Rating schedules with a section for free comments give every
student an opportunity to state what they think and feel and you an
opportunity to compile the overall reactions of the class (some examples
of rating schedules are given in Appendix D). Bradbury and Ramsden
(1975), Black and Rutherford (1975) and Elton (1975) discuss ways of
developing and using schedules for obtaining students' reactions to lectures, and Flood-Page (1974) reviews studies of student evaluations of
teaching in the United States.

Although students' reactions to a lecture are useful indications of its
success, they must be treated with caution, since ratings of lectures are
determined only in part by the lecturer's performance. The other deter-
mining factors are the students' personalities, aptitudes, attitudes and
values. For example, students who scored high on scales of dogmatism express particularly strong preferences for clearcut, easy-to-note presentations

(Smithers, 1970a and b). Those who appear to need more than average social approval stress the importance of warmth and friendliness (White and Wash, 1966. Yes, those are their names). You cannot please all of the students all of the time.

Since personality and subject choice are linked (Entwistle, Percy and Nisbet, 1971), one would also expect students' reactions within different subjects to vary. What may be thought to be good in the arts may be regarded with suspicion in the physical sciences (Riley, Ryan and Lifshitz, 1969).

However, most students appear to value enthusiasm and systematic presentation (Flood-Page, 1974). It is also likely that most of them form their impressions of technique quickly and tend to stick to their initial ones. Kohlan (1973) found that 68 per cent of the variance in a set of ratings could be attributed to the first set of ratings given by students. In less precise, but perhaps more meaningful, terms, first impressions accounted for two-thirds of later ones – they really did count.

It is sometimes argued that students' evaluations of lectures are an irrelevance, that what matters is what they learn, not what they feel. Such a view implies a narrow conception of learning. Attitudes as well as knowledge and skills may be acquired in lectures, and attitudes are partly based on cumulative reactions to lectures and lecture courses. If a student learns basic statistical computations in a lecture course, but also learns to hate statistics, then I would argue that the course had failed. Conversely, if a student enjoyed a lecture course in statistics but did not learn any statistics, then I would still argue the same thing. Which do you think is *most* important for a lecturer to accomplish in a lecture course: the acquisition of favourable attitudes by his students towards a subject or the acquisition of knowledge and skills?

ACTIVITY 37 – Using students' reactions

Prepare, design and give a lecture. Afterwards, ask the class each to complete a rating form (see Appendix D for a selection). Collect the forms, analyse the comments and compile the group totals for each item on the schedule. Analyse your 'perceived' strengths and weaknesses. If you are a member of a group of young lecturers, report on and discuss the students' reactions to your lecture and what steps you propose to take, if any, to modify your lecturing technique. Repeat this activity towards the end of the course and compare the results of the first and second attempts. You may, if you wish, ask students to give their names on the rating schedules: this will enable you to compare the reactions of different groups within the lecture class, such as those of high, medium and low achievers; or of men and women.

MEASURING STUDENTS' UNDERSTANDING OF A LECTURE

Measuring understanding is a complex business. Dressel (1976), Hall (1975), Heywood (1977) and Thyne (1974) discuss the issue and provide some hints on constructing examinations and tests.

A simple and useful way of measuring student understanding is to set a multiple-choice test on three or four of the most important points in lectures. It could contain three types: points requiring (a) *recall* of principles, (b) *identification* of them in other contexts and (c) their *application* to new problems. These are not likely to fit all lecture topics but it should be possible in most subjects to set items which demand high-level thinking or critical responses – at least in some lectures. Even if you have doubts about the use of multiple-choice items in examinations, it may be worth trying some out at the end of a lecture, as this may help you to clarify the important points of your lecture. The analysis of students' results provides you with a guide to what students may have learned. The guide may be imperfect, but it *is* a guide.

ACTIVITY 38 – Attending to a lecture

Prepare and design a lecture. Identify three or four central points in it and draw up a couple of multiple-choice items on each of them. Having delivered the lecture, give out the multiple-choice test. Make sure you allow sufficient time for it to be completed, marked and collected (10 minutes). Give out the answers so that the students may mark their own papers. Stress that you are interested in the class's reponses and not those of individual students: they need not give their names. Collect the test sheets and analyse the results. Obtain the average class score and range for each item. Note any common errors or weaknesses in the students' responses.

ANALYSING LECTURES

The methods and skills of lecturing have been tackled in this and the previous Unit and you have also been introduced to a way of analysing the structure of explanations. You are therefore relatively well-equipped for the task of analysing lectures. Two activities are suggested below. Both are particularly concerned with the structure of lectures, although in carrying them out you will also increase your knowledge of stylistic features and skills.

ACTIVITY 39 – Observing a lecture

Ask a colleague who is reputed to be a good lecturer if you may attend one of his lectures and take notes on the content for use in a small-group discussion. Beforehand find out what the topic is and, if possible, how he proposes to tackle it. If you are not familiar with the topic read (a little) about it.

During the lecture listen and take brief notes so that you can produce a one-page summary of its structure similar to those shown in figs. 6–15. Pay particular attention to the orientation and summary and to the links, if any, between the various parts of the lecture. Prepare the one-page summary and write a brief comment on the structure and any particularly outstanding features. Present the structure, outline the topic (very briefly) and give your comments to members of your group. If possible provide each of them with a copy of the lecture summary. Together summarise the main structure, outstanding features and weaknesses you have all observed and analysed in the lectures you attended.

ACTIVITY 40 – Analysing a lecture

Prepare, give and audio-record a lecture (a radio microphone should be used if possible and, if not, a small microphone clipped to your clothes). Transcribe three sections of the lecture, each of five minutes' duration (beginning, middle and end); leave two margins and double spacing. Insert hesitations and stumbles and the use of audiovisual aids, including the blackboard. Divide the transcript into orientation, mid-sections and summary. Compare the relevant sections of your lecture notes with the transcript and note any major discrepancies. Prepare a brief report on the main features of the analysis and discuss them with members of your group.

Note: this activity is time-consuming but very revealing. You might, if you wish, obtain student ratings on the same lecture and

their responses to a simple achievement test. The three sets of findings could then be compared. Obviously, rigorous comparison would
mean using a transcript of the whole lecture, and it would take
sixteen hours to transcribe and analyse. This is not recommended!

You might also repeat the activity with another lecture or, if
possible, the same lecture given to a different class of students, and
compare the analyses.

Planning a series of lectures

This section provides a series of hints on planning a series of lectures.
They are primarily intended for young lecturers who are tackling the
problem for the first time. The section is not a survey of course design
and evaluation or of curriculum development – interested readers are
referred to Beard (1976), Bligh *et al.* (1975) and Golby *et al.* (1975) for
information on these subjects. Instead, there are a few practical suggestions
which may help a young lecturer who has been given a lecture class,
and perhaps a syllabus, and has been told to lecture. These suggestions
are akin to those in the section on planning a lecture.

There are six basic questions to answer when designing a series of
lectures:

1 What are the constraints on the lecture course?
2 What content shall I teach (and not teach)?
3 What important points and principles do I want the students to learn?
4 What methods shall I use?
5 What is the most appropriate order of topics?
6 How shall I evaluate the course?

Rather than attempt to answer each of these questions in turn, it is
better to zigzag from one to another. You might also consider further
ones, such as 'Why am I teaching this?', 'How important is this?', 'Can I
change the constraints on this lecture course?' It is worth remembering
that just as the way in which a complex scientific experiment is carried
out may bear little relationship to the way in which it is presented in a
journal, so the process of designing a course of lectures may bear little
resemblance to how it is presented in a course outline or handbook.

THE CONSTRAINTS OF THE COURSE

This is perhaps the most appropriate starting point for planning a series
of lectures. Answers are needed to such questions as:

How many hours' contact time? What type of contact (large lecture groups only, lectures and seminars, etc.)? How many students? What are the facilities in the teaching room? What other equipment and resources are available? What can you *safely* assume that the students know? What courses have they already completed? What courses will they be doing at the same time as yours? What courses afterwards? What texts and journals are available in the library? What texts can be bought? Will the students be able to afford them? How many assignments and examinations should be set? When? What proportion of the marks, if any, should contribute to the degree classification? Can you use multiple-choice tests? When should you return the marked work to the students?

The answers to all of these questions shape, inevitably, the design and teaching of the course. There is little point in showing videotapes if students will not be able to see them because of the layout of the room. There is little point in planning several small-group activities if the only room available has tiers of fixed benches. There is little point in setting three long essays per term if you have a class of 250 (if each of the students wrote 16,000 words, you would have four million to read and mark!). These and associated points should be borne in mind when considering the remaining five of the six basic questions involved when planning a series of lectures.

CONTENT, OBJECTIVES, METHODS, ORDER AND EVALUATION

Some writers (e.g. Mager, 1962; Tyler, 1969; Tyler, 1954) suggest that we should begin planning a course by specifying objectives. This is only possible after much experience since it requires a firm grasp of the subject, considerable expertise in teaching and an intimate knowledge of the kinds of students who are taking the course (see Macdonald-Ross, 1973, for a discussion).

Instead of beginning with the question, 'What important points and principles do I want the students to learn?', it is probably better to begin with 'What content shall I teach?' To answer this, I suggest that you look through a few standard texts on the subject of the lecture course and note the headings and sub-headings of their authors. Then free-associate (see Activity 32) and collect clusters of topics. Decide which of these are most important and which may be omitted. Use the free-association sheet to choose an order of topics, prepare a rough draft of this and note any key references which you wish students to read. Note on separate sheets any activities that students might be asked to carry out, any ideas for student assignments and any resources or lecture methods you might use.

After completing the draft, decide what important points and principles you would like the students to learn. Compare them with the draft of the course outline and the lists of possible activities and assignments. Look at the six basic questions on planning a series of lectures and your answers. If you are reasonably satisfied, prepare a course outline which includes these answers. Use this as a working document for preparing your lectures. You might also prepare a course outline for the students so that they have a clear idea of how it is structured, a realistic set of readings and the assignments which are expected of them.

During a course it is sometimes helpful to have brief informal discussions with students on the lecture content and topics. You might also prepare evaluation sheets for use by them at the end of the course. The information obtained from the course evaluation sheets, the students' assignments and your own observations will help you to replan for a more effective course.

ACTIVITY 41 – A problem of integration

This is best carried out in small groups drawn from different disciplines.

Imagine that you are members of an interdisciplinary team who have been asked to prepare a draft outline of a course of ten lectures to a group of 100 first-year students drawn from several disciplines. The lectures do not have any supporting seminars or problem-solving classes. You may assume that there are adequate resources and that the lecture room is well-designed.

Your task is, within one hour, to prepare a draft outline on *one* of the following subjects.

1 Some modern thinkers.
2 Measurement in science.
3 Symbolism.
4 Measurement in social science.
5 Culture.
6 Computers and society.

Use the suggestions in this section of the Unit to complete the task. At the end of the hour, one member of the team should prepare a presentation of the course outline. The teams should then meet as a lecture class and each course outline should be presented. When they have all been discussed, each small group (team) within the class should decide together which outline appeared to be the best and why. The class should then discuss briefly what it has learned from the activity, and the whole thing should be summarised by the class organiser.

Summary

This Unit has been concerned with learning to lecture. It has provided hints and suggestions on preparing, giving and evaluating lectures and a series of activities which may have helped you to develop new strategies of lecturing or to refine existing ones. All the hints and suggestions here have been discussed and used by lecturers who participated in courses on explaining and lecturing. They are guidelines – not rigid prescriptions – which lecturers considered most useful.

Unit Six – Helping students learn from lectures

Study consists essentially in propounding questions to oneself and then trying to solve them. This rhythm of question and answer runs throughout all learning and all teaching. (Hamilton, 1928)

Most students on degree courses spend 400 hours in lectures, so it does not seem unreasonable to spend three or four hours in helping them to gain more from these lectures. This Unit, accordingly, contains information, hints and activities on ways of doing this. It is based on a training programme developed with students at a university and at a polytechnic (Brown, 1978b). Having read it and thought about the suggestions, you should be able to devise a programme which will help students to learn more efficiently and effectively from lectures – provided also that they are prepared to help themselves.

If you have read the previous Units and have carried out the activities in them, then you are already in a good position to help students. You can outline to them a simple model of learning from lectures (fig. 3, p. 44), and point out that such learning involves listening, observing, summarising and note-taking *during* a lecture, and note-making, learning and thinking *afterwards*. You can identify the various methods of lecturing and the difficulties that they present to learners. You can discuss with students your own techniques of lecturing and, if you wish, the problems they may encounter in learning from your lectures. You can show them transcripts of explanations and give them practice in note-taking from a transcript. You could also show them what you consider to be 'good' and 'bad' examples of notes either taken during a lecture or made afterwards.

This last sort of information is perhaps most valuable to first-year students, though not all final-year ones are efficient at note-taking.

Incidentally, it is worth remembering that first-year students of your subject are more like first-year students of other subjects than they are like third-year ones of your own subject.

These simple points will almost certainly help first-year students to learn from lectures but, if you want to develop their learning strategies more fully, you and they must invest a few hours of time and effort in the task. The rest of this Unit will help you in that direction – it consists of hints and suggestions on preparing to learn from lectures, on listening and observing during them, on note-taking, on note-making and on learning afterwards.

PREPARING TO LEARN

Just as reading is more productive if one knows what to look for in the text, so is learning from lectures. Hence the first step is to prepare to learn. This means that a student must perform two tasks: first, he must refresh his knowledge of the topic by quickly reviewing notes made from the previous lecture and from relevant books; second, just before the lecture begins, he must jot down questions which he thinks might be covered in the lecture. The first task requires a good filing system. The second task is obviously impossible if students do not know what topic will be dealt with. Students able to perform both tasks have reported that they found note-taking easier. The questions they scribbled before the lecture helped them to anticipate the significant points in it. This also helped them to detect important questions which they had not considered.

Amongst other things, this advice to students means that the lecturer needs to inform them of the topics of each lecture. This can be done by giving them an outline of the lecture course.

How much to note?

This is a question often asked by students but, not surprisingly, there are no precise answers to it. Some lecturers prefer to give massive coverage of a topic without indicating important points, others to explore ideas at random and aloud, and others to outline coherently facts, ideas and theories. Students therefore have to decide whether to listen, observe and scribble; to listen, observe, select and note; to listen, observe, understand and take fewer notes; or just to listen.

Furthermore, if a lecturer delivers information at breakneck speed, students may have to form a syndicate to catch the information. If he is very slow, they may have to do the same to keep awake. Between these two extremes there has to be a decision on how much to note. The best general strategy is, probably, to listen, observe, try to understand and to take brief notes. Listening and observing in lectures are crucial, but neglected, skills, and it is worth spending time on helping students to develop them.

Listening and observing

During lectures a student can look out for various gambits used in them. This search sharpens listening and observing, and also helps him to think along with the lecturer and to try to anticipate the *kinds* of statement the latter is about to make. Two gambits are particularly worth exploring: moves and modes. Moves are the way in which a lecturer switches from one section of a lecture to another; modes are the kinds of discourse he uses – defining, designating, explaining, etc.

MOVES IN DISCOURSE

In a recent experiment I taught groups of students to categorise types of discourse. They practised on tapescripts and videotaped explanations, and their first task was to learn this simple category system:

Preambles   Ritualistic mutterings such as 'um – er – good afternoon. Today we are – er – going to – er – consider – um – an – er – important – er – topic.'

Orientation   The framework of the lecture. Needless to say, some lecturers do not make this explicit. Ideally, they state what they are going to talk about and write headings down. Orientations may occur at the beginning of a lecture or at the beginning of topics or subtopics (see next).

Frames   The framing of the subtopics in a lecture. They usually begin with such words as 'Now ...', 'So far ...', 'This then ...', Sometimes the lecturer simply pauses and looks down at his notes. The 'framing words' indicate a switch in topic. What immediately follows a frame is usually (not always) important.

Keys   Key statements. These are central principles, rules, facts, conjectures or questions. Watch out for them. The questions you have scribbled down will probably alert you to them.

Examples   These may be examples of the principles or facts, or may be metaphors, illustrations and analogies. A *brief* note of them will help you to understand the principle.

Summaries   These may occur at the end of topics or subtopics as well as at the end of a lecture.

Learning the category system did improve the students' listening and note-taking. They found the various kinds of framing move to be particularly helpful. So here are further examples of different kinds of framing which have been observed in lectures:

'*Today I am going to talk about* animal locomotion *with particular reference* to felines' [Orientation to lecture easily missed].

'*Now* [pause] *let's look more closely at* Tinbergen's view of ...' [Further detail and criticisms coming].

'*Now you might ask why* Linnaeus's original classification system is important' [orientation – reasons coming].

'*However, not all* findings fit this model' [qualifications to main point coming].

'*Moreover, this view was not only shared by* nineteenth-century historians, *it was also* ...' [orientation – a supporting point likely to be made].

'*On the other hand* ...' [alternative view coming].

'*So, job evaluation is* ...' [summary or definition coming].

'*Thus we can see* ...' [summary or conclusion coming].

'*The main point is* ...' [clarification, summary or main point is coming].

'*What I am trying to say is* ...' [classification, summary or main point may be coming].

'*So far we have looked at* ...' [summary and new topic coming].

'*Let's look at* ...' [new topic coming].

'*Here then is a second equation*' [new topic coming].

'*However, that's not very important*' [an aside has just been made and you may have thought it was important].

'*Well, that's what x* [an author] *said about this. However I'm not going to talk about that today. What I propose to do* ...' [an irrelevance has just been given and it fooled you].

'*This then is the important point*' [a key point perhaps coming].

'*Despite reservations the main finding appears to be* ...' [a key point].

Students found that these framing moves were useful signposts in discourse. They also found useful some demonstrations of the non-verbal cues which accompany framing and focusing moves. Here are some common ones:

Lecturer writes on board	[next section or just lecturer restlessness?].
Lecturer steps back from board and stares at it	[Just checking].
Lecturer removes spectacles	[probably a main point coming].
Lecturer removes spectacles and pauses	[probably a qualification or reservation].
Lecturer stares out of window	[lecturer thinking of what to say; maybe a pretty girl passing by].
Lecturer raises finger	[qualification coming].
Lecturer closes hand and gestures	[probably an important point coming].
Lecturer uses 'halt' sign	[qualification coming].
Lecturer looks at notes	[next section coming or he is lost].
Lecturer stares hard at notes	[he is lost].
Lecturer scrambles through transparencies	[he is lost].
Lecturer looks up from notes and stops reading	[he is about to explain a point; usually important].
Lecturer sits on desk and lights a cigarette	[you are about to be given the 'I'm a good guy' technique? Maybe a substitute for a lecture – but not always].

These are simple points but no less helpful for that. They may be supplemented with further examples of non-verbal cues from previous Units in this book and from your own observations.

However, everyone uses speech and non-verbal cues in an individual way, so it is important, too, for students to study a lecturer's style of presentation. Since there is no guarantee that lectures will be clearly structured and interestingly expressed, some training in listening for common errors was also given. One of the most common is for a lecturer to begin a section of a lecture with several qualifications and reservations before making the main point. Since the listeners do not know what the main point is, these are relatively meaningless.

Another common error is the 'pseudo-link' – the lecturer appears to be linking what he has said in a previous section or lecture with what he is going to talk about next, but he never says what the next section is about. A third common error is for a lecturer to evaluate a main point before he indicates what it is.

All these errors were labelled by one student as 'forms of backward-lecturing'. They may be signals of inadequate preparation. Before reading on, lecturers and students might like to consider the question: 'How can one take reasonable notes from backward-lecturing?'

MODES OF DISCOURSE

The verbal and non-verbal moves signpost the discourse. The discourse itself may be classified into types of explaining, and this, in turn, helps to improve listening and note-taking. The main types of explaining are, as we have seen: descriptive – what happens, how things are made; interpretative – what is ...?'; and reason-giving – answers to questions which usually begin with 'Why?'

Asking oneself in a lecture whether the lecturer is describing, interpreting or reason-giving directs one's listening and observing. This, in its turn, helps one to decide whether a note is necessary. When one can do this quickly, one can also try to decide which of the following a lecturer is doing.

Cognitive modes   Possible clue

(Is the lecturer ...?)

Defining?   'X may be defined/regarded/described as ....'.
                   'We call this ...'.
                   'This is a form of ...'.

Designating?   Designation is essentially labelling – assigning names.

Describing?   No obvious common clue: the lecturer may describe
                   events, processes, procedures, phenomena, views.

Classifying?   'There are n types of ...' (n is frequently 3).

Stating?   No common clue: is the statement put forward as a
                   fact, opinion, assumption, axiom or as a basic concept?

Reporting?   'The main findings were ...'.
                   'His views were ...'.

Comparing and contrasting?	'These ... share common characteristics.'
	'These ... have certain affinities.'
	'However, there are distinctive differences ...'.
Evaluating?	'So what does this mean ...?'
	'But, how important ...'.
	'Let us explore the merits of ...'.
	'The main conclusions one can drawn from this study are ...'.
Conditionally inferring?	'If.... then ...'.

Obviously it is not enough to tell students these categories, they must also have practice in identifying them in tapescripts of explanations and excerpts from lectures.

Training in moves and modes seems to sharpen perception of discourse and to make note-taking easier. But the training is intended only to help students to improve their listening and observing. The moves and modes are not categories for note-taking.

Note-taking in lectures

Listening and note-taking is much harder than reading and note-taking. One can backtrack and compare parts of a book but the only person who can backtrack easily in a lecture is the lecturer. Most of us can only recall about twenty words without processing them and, whilst we are doing so, we may not be listening attentively.

Despite these difficulties, the aim of note-taking in lectures is to produce easy-to-read outlines which can be worked on afterwards. Here are a few simple general hints which students have found helpful.

1 Put the date and subject on the first sheet, and number subsequent sheets.
2 Leave plenty of space between notes and have wide margins so that, if necessary, inserts can be made later in the lecture or afterwards.
3 Use capitals for main sections, underline headings of subsections and common key words.
4 Use abbreviations such as 'i.e.', 'e.g.', 'N.B.', and make up your own abbreviations of frequently used words (do not use these abbreviations in course work or exams).
5 Use arrows, decision trees, flow charts and Venn diagrams.
6 Separate main points, supporting reasons, examples and qualifications. Some students find the use of 'P', 'R', 'E' and 'Q' helpful in this connection.

7 When a lecturer shows a complex diagram and talks whilst he is doing so, decide which – words or diagram – matters most. If the diagram is very important, ask him to wait (it is better if several students do this, rather than one). Simplify the diagram if you can. Circles, arrows and abbreviations are useful in flow charts and models. If the lecturer is showing a very complex structure which is available in a book, do not attempt to copy it but, instead, follow and note his explanation.

8 Sometimes you may need to get down a definition verbatim, or a process formula or the steps of a proof which are not readily available in textbooks. Use as many abbreviations as possible. Compare notes of these immediately after the lecture. Ask the lecturer to clarify difficult points – if he is amenable to questioning.

9 Try to listen, anticipate and follow the structure of the lecture rather than to take copious notes. Grains of understanding are worth more than sheaves of lecture notes.

What other advice would you give your students? What would you suggest they do in a lecture if the lecturer spends most of the time writing notes on the board? What would you suggest they do when the lecturer reads from a prepared script?

Note-making after lectures

The notes *taken* during a lecture are merely an aid to remembering the discourse. At least 60 per cent of a lecture is forgotten within 24 hours unless action is taken (Jones, 1923; Bassey, 1968; McLeish, 1976). If a lecture is worth attending, then it is probably worth *making* notes on and thinking about (this has implications for timetabling private study activities). As far as possible notes should be made on the same day.

Notes taken during a lecture may be disorganised and unclear, so that they need working on. One way of doing this is to try to reconstruct and to analyse the lecture, using the notes taken during it and one's knowledge of lecture methods, modes of discourse and, of course, the subject. Analysis of the structure of lectures is the essential ingredient of note-making and learning from them. The notes made should be based on the hints already given. Unlikely abbreviations, diagrams and important verbatim definitions or proofs should be set out clearly and, perhaps, annotated. The act of note-making is to make the notes permanently memorable, so the use of coloured pens, boxes, arrows, flow diagrams and summary charts are important. The better organised the notes, the easier they are to understand, recall or relearn.

There are two pitfalls in note-making. The first is not to distinguish between key points, subsidiary or supporting points and examples, so that the notes are a bland extensive tabloid rather than a sharply defined cognitive map. A summary chart or diagram forces the note-maker to select, and selection improves his organisation and understanding. The very act of selecting may also raise questions in his mind and may evoke critical comments which should also be noted, summarised and thought over. The second pitfall is to produce a cryptic outline which a week later looks beautiful – but meaningless. The notes made should not only look memorable but should be meaningful.

Learning and thinking about lecture notes

Some students say that note-making after lectures is a waste of time. But, if a lecture is worth attending, it is worth taking notes during it and making notes from it. But that is not enough: what matters is not what is in the notes but what is in the heads of the note-takers. So after making notes one should *always* learn them by trying to recall or reproduce them and applying them to questions in your head such as, 'What are the main points of ...?', 'What are the advantages and disadvantages of ...?', etc. The act of learning notes in this way may require will-power, but it has several advantages. Firstly, it arrests forgetting, secondly it reveals any weaknesses in understanding, thirdly it forces a student to think and organise his knowledge, fourthly it gives practice in applying knowledge, fifthly it increases flexibility of thinking, sixthly it helps a student to see relationships between the content of one lecture, other lectures and his reading, and seventhly it makes revision and writing considerably easier. All this comes from ten to fifteen minutes of learning and thinking *immediately* after note-making. The pay-off is high, the costs relatively trivial.

Discerning readers will have noted that the qualification to all this is 'If a lecture is worth attending'. At the risk of seeming disloyal to my fellow lecturers, some lectures are not worth attending except perhaps for students to meet each other. However, there are dangers in making snap judgements on the value of a particular course of lectures – rationalisations are easy, ratiocinations are less so. When in doubt my advice to students is to attend the lectures and follow through all the steps of learning from lectures.

Eventually a student will find that the notes he takes need very little adjustment after a lecture – but they still need learning and thinking about.

ACTIVITY 42 – Analysing notes

Prepare copies of the tapescripts of explanation given on pages 12–14. Ask the students to read and take notes from them and then to decide which was easier to take notes from and why. They should then form groups of four and each group should compare notes and reasons. Ask each group to state which tapescript was easier, to state one reason why and to give a supporting example.

Introduce the students to framing moves and to the various modes of discourse and then ask them to look for the framing moves in the tapescripts, to examine the orientation and to identify key points, examples, asides and irrelevancies.

ACTIVITY 43 – Making notes

Give a brief explanation of a simple topic or, better still, show a videotaped explanation. Ask the students to take notes and then, in groups of three or four, to compare the layout, structure and content of their notes and then to make a well-structured and meaningful note on the explanation.

Ask two or three groups to show their notes on an overhead projector or blackboard and the remainder of the groups to evaluate them.

ACTIVITY 44 – Noting hints

Show a videotaped explanation and ask the class to take notes from it. Divide the class into groups of three or four and ask them to prepare seven practical specific hints on note-taking. After about ten minutes ask each group to show two of their hints on the blackboard. When all the groups have given two, ask if there are any further hints. Add these to the list together with any you may have thought of yourself. Ask the students to prepare from this list their own set of hints for their own use. Show another videotaped explanation and get them to take notes from that and to check which of their own hints they have followed or not followed.

ACTIVITY 45 – Guided note-taking

Use the material in this section to prepare a guide to learning from lectures which includes examples of poor and good notes taken during a lecture and poor and good ones made after it.

Give a brief explanation of a topic and ask the students to take notes from it, to make a note and to keep it for the next lecture class. Then give out the handout and get them to read it and try the ideas suggested. At the next lecture class give another brief explanation of a topic and ask the students to take notes and make a note. Then ask them to work, in groups of three or four, at comparing and evaluating the notes on both explanations and to suggest to each other ways of improving their note-taking. Towards the end of the session they should discuss briefly amongst themselves the guide which you gave them, and should offer suggestions and comments which, in their view, would improve the guide.

Epilogue – The end of explaining and lecturing

This book has been concerned with explaining and lecturing. In writing it, I had in mind the goal of helping lecturers and students to improve learning from lectures. There are two major strategies that one can adopt for this purpose. The first is to help lecturers to develop their methods of preparing and giving lectures through ideas and activities which increase their awareness of the processes involved. The second is almost the inverse of the first: it is to help students to develop *their* methods of learning from lectures through ideas and activities which increase their awareness of the processes. Both strategies require an understanding of the processes of lecturing and learning from lectures, both require analyses of these processes and practice, and both shaped the structure of the book. The hints, suggestions, information and activities were all geared to helping lecturers and their students to improve learning from lectures.

As for the end of explaining and lecturing, in one sense, they have no end. In another, their end is to convey information, give understanding and generate interest. I hope that this book has helped you towards achieving this end.

Comments and answers on some activities

Activity 1 (p. 3) – What is good teaching in higher education?
Now spend five minutes considering the following question: How far did the notes and presentations in your group embody the characteristics that you consider are important in good teaching in higher education? After all, the medium is sometimes the message. . . .

Most people use the following terms (or equivalent terms) to describe good teachers – well-organised, clear, well-prepared, enthusiastic, interested (in the subject), interested (in the students), friendly, open, flexible, systematic, helpful, committed, creative. 'Well-organised', 'enthusiastic' and 'helpful' are much valued characteristics by students in most subjects. Bear this in mind if you are tempted to say that generalisations on good teaching are impossible!

Activity 3 (p. 10) – Sorting out explanations
Answers (remember that 'what?', 'how?' and 'why?' are only approximations): (1) interpretative; (2) arguable – ostensibly interpretative but also involving description and perhaps reason-giving; (3) descriptive; (4) descriptive; (5) reason-giving masquerading as descriptive; (6) reason-giving; (7) interpretative; (8) reason-giving; (9) interpretative; (10) descriptive; (11) reason-giving; (12) descriptive; (13) the problem is yours; (14) reason-giving. Almost all reason-giving explanations can be regarded as answers to the question 'why?'. Other forms of question requiring a reason-giving explanation can be translated into 'why?'. Interpretative and descriptive explanations shade into one another: 'how' and 'what?' may be used interchangeably. 'How are limits defined?' may look like a descriptive question, but in the form 'What are the various definitions of limits?' it is clearly an interpretative question asking for reports of common usage; (15) interpretative.

Activity 4 (p. 12) – The structure of explanations
It is difficult for most non-biologists to decide what tapescript 1 is about. It contains several hesitations and technical terms and does not appear to answer the question posed in the opening key. The key questions for the two explanations are as follows. Your list may not agree exactly with mine but it should largely do so.

Tapescript 1
Orientation (opening key)
　　Why are nude mice important to biologists? (this is presumably what the explainer intended to explain).
Second Key
　　What is the thymus? Why is it important?
Third Key
　　What happens when the thymus is removed?
Fourth Key
　　How do nude mice come into this?
　　(this is an incomplete key: there is no summary).
The analysis shows that the keys do not explain adequately why nude mice are important to biologists. The explanation could have been improved by statements in the orientation indicating the structure of the explanation. The explainer's second, restructured explanation is as follows.

Tapescript 2
Orientation (opening key)
　　Why are nude mice important to biologists – the absence of thymus not their nudity.
Second Key
　　Why is absence of thymus useful condition?
Third Key
　　Why is 'natural' absence preferable to experimental removal of thymus?
Fourth Key
　　Summary of keys
Notice how the explainer has now provided a set of keys which solve the problem posed. He also used fewer hesitations, technical terms and complex sentences.

Activity 5 (pp. 17–18) – Taking steps
This activity is more difficult than it appears. Literal-minded people often ask for definitions of a 'brief explanation' and 'a group of intelligent

people'. Definitions of these terms are not given, and the participants are asked to decide for themselves. The precise meaning of the question is the next obstacle encountered by some of them, but they must provide their own interpretation. Each of the questions contains several hidden variables and main points, *some* of which are given below. There is unlikely to be perfect agreement on what the important ones are.

1 Ingredients, facilities, power, procedures, precautions.
2 Energy conversion, biochemical reactions, cell generations.
3 The economy consists of industry, commerce, consumers and their interactions. Oil is a source of energy, of raw materials, and of constituents of many products.
4 Plays usually have plots, characters, settings, speech and actions. Are spectators necessary? What are plays for? Are the functions of plays part of their characteristics?
5 Biological – physical, hormonal; social – socialisation processes, stereotyping, social expectations and opportunities.
6 What is teaching? What is teaching in higher education? Is it different from teaching in secondary education? What is good teaching in higher education?
7 Absence of food, moisture, etc. Presence of noxious substances or competing plants. Why does the first cause death? Why does the second cause death.
8 What kinds of jobs? Can one generalise? What counts as success? Psychological characteristics of person. Job characteristics. Match of person to job and vice versa.
9 Main causes and precipitating causes. Main causes may include territory, markets, personal ambitions or paranoia of leaders. Precipitating causes may include border disputes, provocation, internal unrest, etc.
10 To deal with this topic, first formulate the title more precisely: it could be converted to 'What are the stresses and strains in the lives of lecturers?' Then decide whether 'stresses and strains' is a cliché for difficulties or whether it implies two main types of difficulty – pulling outwards, pushing inwards. 'Lecturers' lives' – which lecturers? What does 'lives' consist of? Are the stresses and strains in lecturers' lives different from those of other people?

This activity should have introduced you to the range of hidden variables, main points and their relationship in seemingly simple questions.

Activity 23 (p. 52) – A game of directions
This activity is usually enjoyed by participants. It is lighthearted, but it has a serious intention, since it demonstrates the importance of clarity and order. The activity also indirectly teaches the importance of clarifying the nature of a task. All the tasks look relatively simple until one begins to ask such questions as 'how many?', 'where?', 'what?', 'when?', 'who?' The first step in giving directions is to analyse the task and then redefine it; a second is to consider the resources available. Other steps follow from these.

Appendices

Appendix A – Organising video-recordings

It is important to make the organisation of video-recordings as simple as possible so that recording and viewing can proceed smoothly and without undue delay. High-quality television productions take too long. Television technicians and camera operators can become obsessed with picture quality, whereas the correct focus is the quality of the teaching. Hence it is best to tell the technical staff what you want and do not want and, if possible, to use members of the group or team as camera operators. This has the further merit of encouraging them to look at other's teaching and it shows them that audiovisual equipment is not as formidable as it appears.

The equipment and its use
Fig. 14 shows possible set-ups with one and two cameras. In the one-camera set-up all of the team should be shown how to focus, zoom, pan and track, and they should usually be asked to focus on the 'lecturer' (and his blackboard, diagrams, etc.) but to intersperse with shots of the rest of the group during the explaining and lecturing activities. Occasional close-ups of the face, the hands, and even the feet of the lecturer are sometimes revealing, as are occasional ones of the students.

In the two-camera set-up it may be necessary to use fixed camera positions and for the person acting as operator to select and record pictures using the control gear. If a split screen is available, it should be used to show the 'lecturer' or 'student' who is speaking and the students or lecturer who are listening. If there are more than seven people in the group, then each person can act as camera operator 1 and 2 and also as the selector. For the activities on explaining and lecturing, a one-camera set-up with five or six team members is better than a two-

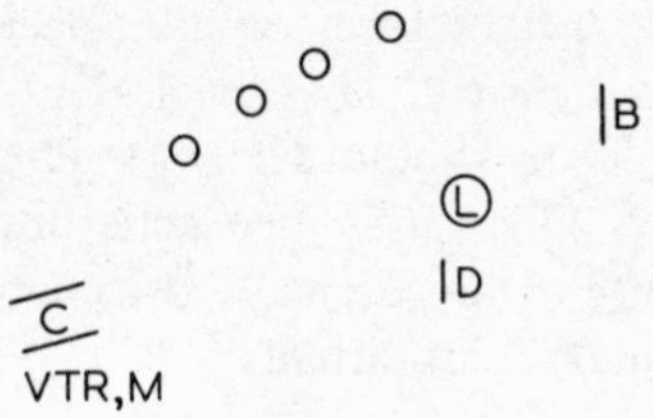

(a) A one-camera set-up

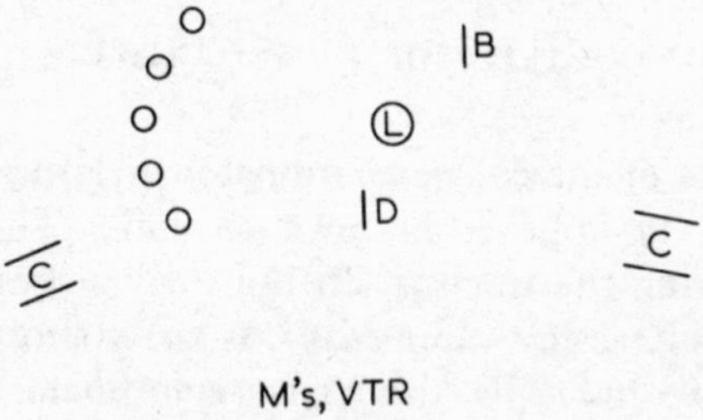

(b) A two–camera set-up

Fig. 14

B = blackboard and overhead projector; C = camera; D = desk; L = person acting as lecturer; M = monitor; O = person acting as student; VTR = videotape recorder.

Note: The monitors should be turned away from the 'lecturers' and 'students', otherwise they may be distracted by the sight of themselves. The sound on the monitors should be turned down while recording in order to avoid echo.

camera set-up with seven or more. The two–camera set-up is better for seminar and tutorial practice.

In both set-ups it is best to use a clip microphone. This cuts down excessive sound interference, and sound is more difficult to record than vision. If this is not possible the microphone should be suspended over the heads of the group. The rooms in which the recordings are made should be seminar rooms (6m × 8m) rather than lecture theatres. They should be well lit and ventilated and, if possible, carpeted. The chairs and desks should be light and movable, and there should be a black or white board plus chalk, pens and cleaners, and an overhead projector. The lightweight, silent overhead projector is preferable because it does not make a noise and its illumination is not as intense. Before beginning a recording session, check that pictures on the blackboard and overhead projector may be recorded clearly. Also check the sound quality.

Each member of the team should act as 'student', camera operator, timekeeper and 'lecturer'. This varies their activities and enables them to observe teaching from different positions. It also enables them to see others teach – a rare event in higher education.

Appendix B – The role of the course coordinator and group leaders in courses for new lecturers

Put simply, the role of the course coordinator or group leader is to help the young lecturer to improve his own teaching. Their role therefore changes subtly during the training. In the early stages they need to be particularly encouraging and supportive. As the young lecturer learns to analyse and improve his skills, the course coordinator should gradually withdraw his support – but not his encouragement. By the end of the training programme a young lecturer should be able to analyse his own teaching and suggest improvements without any help from the course coordinator. In short, the latter should try to work himself out of a job and the young lecturer into fully fledged membership of a profession.

Beginners in almost any training situation need to be given the opportunity to try out ideas as well as hints and guidelines for themselves. There are arguments, however, about the relative amounts of freedom or direction to be given. Some prefer to adopt Rogers' approach of non-directive counselling (Rogers, 1969) but in so doing they may be abrogating their role. As trainers, others may prefer to issue rigid directives. The first may lead to change but not in the most fruitful directions: the change may include the total rejection of valuable help and the adoption of teaching strategies known to be rotten. The second may lead to superficial compliance followed by a total rejection of the ideas after formal training has been completed. Maier (1958) dubs these strategies 'listen' and 'tell' in his text on appraisal interviews. His third strategy, 'Listen-and-Tell', allows young lecturers to analyse their own skills and to suggest their own approaches; at the same time the course coordinator or group leader is perceived as a helpful guide and he can offer prompts, hints and suggestions. The suggestions below contain a few ideas about the technique.

As far as possible, the course coordinator or group leader should open the discussion with the question, 'Well [person's name], what did you think of that?' The group member should be encouraged to indicate the positive parts of his attempt as well as its weaknesses and to suggest ways of improving on what he did. The other members should then be asked for their comments and suggestions. They may be reluctant to give this initially. At the end of the discussion of a member's activity the course coordinator or group leader should summarise the main points made and offer one or two hints (but no more than that) of his own.

If this is a first venture into training with videotape feedback, then the course coordinator should have a preliminary meeting with group leaders to discuss methods of observing and discussing videotape. This is a sensitive area and requires delicate handling. Coordinators might like to try the Listen-and-Tell approach in this task.

SUGGESTIONS FOR GROUP LEADERS

Group leaders are asked to meet the members of their group to discuss the videotaped activities. Please follow the instructions for each activity and use the guidelines, rating schedule and analytical procedures which have been provided.

When commenting upon a young lecturer's performance you are particularly asked to adopt the following procedure.

1 Know the names of the members of the group.
2 Read the activity and associated material before viewing.
3 Begin each viewing session with a question such as 'Well, what did you think of that?'
4 Use prompts, gentle probes and questions to encourage the young lecturer to give the good as well as the weak points and to suggest improvements.
5 Ask other members of the group for their opinions and suggestions.
6 Give one or two hints on *important* points which the team may have omitted.
7 Summarise the group's views and suggestions, including your own.

Remember: A main objective of the discussion sessions is to make the task of analysing and improving teaching a rewarding experience for the young lecturer rather than an exercise in fault-finding by the group leader. You may if you wish audio-record or video-record a discussion session to check on your strategies of handling it.

Before leaving this topic it may be as well to discuss the apparent contradiction between the use of hints and guidelines for the activities given in this book and the counselling approach recommended for the discussion sessions. The contradiction is, however, superficial. Both are based upon the principle that positive reinforcement and feedback improve learning. The use of a young lecturer's ideas by a group leader in discussion is itself rewarding and encourages the former to supply further analyses and suggestions. Thus by listening, gently probing, summarising and telling, the group leader uses a powerful technique to direct the lecturer's attention to his central task: improving his own teaching. At the same time the lecturer is likely to make detailed suggestions which he thinks he can carry out. The same suggestions from a group leader might appear to the lecturer to be beyond his capabilities.

Appendix C – Organising short courses

It is not proposed to describe in detail how to organise short courses on explaining and lecturing. But the following general points may be useful to intending organisers.

1 Prepare a course outline for participants and group leaders which sets out clearly the objectives of the course, the activities and a timetable.
2 Check that all equipment is working and that all teaching rooms are fully equipped.
3 Check that meals and drinks are available for participants.
4 Check that materials, paper, pens, etc., are available.
5 Provide a booklet of information on the course or paginated references to this book (or other ones). At the end of the course provide an opportunity for discussion of it.
6 Stick closely to the course timetable.

These points may seem simple and obvious, yet courses often founder because of lack of attention to them.

This book provides a wide range of materials and activities which could be used on short courses. The following are just a selection:

One-day course on explaining. This could centre on preparing, giving and analysing explanations. Activities 2, 4, 9 and 12 could be used. It is important to leave sufficient free time between Activities 2 and 12 for the participants to redesign an explanation or prepare a new explanation. The course is best done as an afternoon session followed by a morning session on the next day.

One-day course on lecturing. This could centre on ways of preparing and

giving lectures. Activity 4 (tapescript analysis) demonstrates the importance of structure: Activities 31, 32 and 33 could also be used.

One-day course on evaluating lectures. This could be based on some of
Activities 34–40. Participants could be asked to try some of them *before*
coming on the course. Alternatively the course could be organised as two
half-days separated by a week.

One-day course on learning from lectures. This could be based upon
Activity 4 plus modified forms of Activities 42–6.

Two-day course on explaining and lecturing. Of several possible courses,
only one example is given here. A course based on Activities 2, 4, 9, 12,
31, 32, 33 is a useful basic one. On a residential course, the first
evening could be devoted to Activities 14, 20 and 21. The second evening
should be set aside for private study and informal discussion groups.

Appendix D – Examples of rating schedules

Three examples of rating schedules are given. The first has been used by
lecturers at the University of Nottingham and the second by lecturers at
the North London Polytechnic. The third example is taken from the lecture
feedback package prepared by Vivian Hodgson and David McConnell of
the Institute of Educational Technology, University of Surrey. Further
information about it may be obtained from: The Administrative Assistant,
Institute of Educational Technology, University of Surrey, Guildford,
G02 5XH.

COURSE EVALUATION SHEET - LECTURING

This schedule is part of a series which has been designed to help us evaluate and monitor courses. This will help us to modify existing courses and develop new ones. This schedule is concerned with the lecture. Please rate the lecture *you have just received* on the items below.

Please indicate the following:

Subject .... Topic ....

Year (1st, 2nd or 3rd etc.) ..... Today's date ....

Give your reaction to each separate item on the Yes/No and 6 point scales below. Do not omit any item.

6 = very highly favourable   3 = slightly unfavourable
5 = highly favourable   2 = unfavourable
4 = favourable   1 = extremely unfavourable

Put a ring round the boxes which most clearly describe your view on that item.

		Yes	No					
1.	The lecture was clearly structured.			6	5	4	3	2	1
2.	The lecturer indicated when he had come to the end of a major section.			6	5	4	3	2	1
3.	The main points given were clear and understandable.			6	5	4	3	2	1
4.	The minor points and reservations given were understandable and clear.			6	5	4	3	2	1
5.	The examples given were relevant.			6	5	4	3	2	1
6.	The examples given were interesting.			6	5	4	3	2	1
7.	The pace (speed) of the lecture was right for me.			6	5	4	3	2	1
8.	The amount of material covered was right for me.			6	5	4	3	2	1
9.	The lecture was clearly audible.			6	5	4	3	2	1
10.	The blackboard and other aids were used effectively.			6	5	4	3	2	1
11.	The lecture seemed well prepared.			6	5	4	3	2	1
12.	The lecture was well presented.			6	5	4	3	2	1
13.	The lecture held my attention most of the time.			6	5	4	3	2	1
14.	The lecture was interesting.			6	5	4	3	2	1
15.	The lecturer usually looked at and talked to the lecture group and not to the furniture fittings.			6	5	4	3	2	1
16.	The lecturer summarised the main points of the lecture effectively.			6	5	4	3	2	1

Write here a brief general comment on the lecture:

Thank you for your help. Please return this form immediately to the lecturer.

NORTH EAST LONDON POLYTECHNIC STUDENT FEEDBACK PROJECT

CONTACT PHIL BRADBURY

PLEASE READ CAREFULLY BEFORE YOU ANSWER THE QUESTIONNAIRE

Your lecturer would like to know your views on his or her teaching. Knowledge of your opinions could help to plan future classes, to avoid unnecessary misunderstandings, and to improve staff-student relationships.

Please use Section I of the Questionnaire to make your opinions known. Read each of the statements carefully and indicate whether you agree or disagree with it as a description of this lecturer's teaching. You should do this by circling the number opposite each statement which most nearly corresponds to your view.

Take into account all aspects of the lecturer's teaching with which you are familiar, whether it is lectures, seminars, practical work, etc. or any combination of these.

When you have completed this, please fill in Section II of the Questionnaire (on the back page), to help us establish the relative importance of each of the statements. In this case, please indicate how important you think each of the statements is for this course.

In all cases, please give your own opinion and be as honest as possible. This questionnaire is absolutely *ANONYMOUS*.

PLEASE DO NOT WRITE EITHER YOUR NAME OR THAT OF YOUR LECTURER ANY-WHERE ON THIS FORM.

Section I : Feedback Questionnaire

Please indicate, by circling the appropriate number in each case, your agreement or disagreement with each of the following statements:

The Lecturer	Strongly Disagree	Disagree	Neither Agree Nor Disagree	Agree	Strongly Agree
1. Is clear and understandable in his or her explanations	1	2	3	4	5
2. Stimulates students to think independently	1	2	3	4	5
3. Makes a genuine effort to get students involved in discussion	1	2	3	4	5
4. Presents material in a well-organised way	1	2	3	4	5
5. Makes good use of handouts eg duplicated lecture notes, examples of problems, reading lists	1	2	3	4	5
6. Is sensitive to the feelings and problems of individual students	1	2	3	4	5
7. Is enthusiastic about his or her subject	1	2	3	4	5
8. Stresses important material	1	2	3	4	5
9. Makes constructive and helpful comments on written work	1	2	3	4	5
10. Adjusts his or her pace to the needs of the class	1	2	3	4	5
11. Gives a good factual coverage of the subject matter	1	2	3	4	5
12. Shows a good sense of humour	1	2	3	4	5
13. Writes legibly on the blackboard	1	2	3	4	5
14. Returns written work promptly	1	2	3	4	5
15. Shows a thorough knowledge of his or her subject	1	2	3	4	5
16. Shows the relevance of his or her subject to the work you expect to do when you qualify	1	2	3	4	5
17. Points out the links between his or her subject and related subjects	1	2	3	4	5
18. Is readily accessible to students outside formal classes	1	2	3	4	5
19. Encourages students to express their own opinions	1	2	3	4	5
20. Is always well prepared for his or her classes	1	2	3	4	5
21. Is punctual and reliable in his or her attendance	1	2	3	4	5
22. Tries to link lecture material to laboratory work/practical work/seminars	1	2	3	4	5
23. Can be clearly heard	1	2	3	4	5

On how many previous occasions have you completed the NELP Student Feedback Questionnaire (for this lecturer or any other)   0   1   2   3+

Section II :   Importance Ratings

Please indicate how important *you think it is that lecturers teaching*
on this course should show each of the following characteristics.
Do this by circling the appropriate number on the five point scale
(ie 1 if you think the characteristic is of little *importance and*
so on up to 5 if you think it is of great *importance).*

Lecturers on this course	Of Little Importance				Of Great Importance
1. Should be clear and understandable in their explanations	1	2	3	4	5
2. Should stimulate students to think independently	1	2	3	4	5
3. Should make a genuine effort to get students involved in discussion	1	2	3	4	5
4. Should present material in a well-organised way	1	2	3	4	5
5. Should make good use of handouts eg duplicated lecture notes, examples of problems, reading lists	1	2	3	4	5
6. Should be sensitive to the feelings and problems of individual students	1	2	3	4	5
7. Should be enthusiastic about their subject	1	2	3	4	5
8. Should stress important material	1	2	3	4	5
9. Should make constructive and helful comments on written work	1	2	3	4	5
10. Should adjust their pace to the needs of the class	1	2	3	4	5
11. Should give a good factual coverage of the subject matter	1	2	3	4	5
12. Should show a good sense of humour	1	2	3	4	5
13. Should write legibly on the blackboard	1	2	3	4	5
14. Should return written work promptly	1	2	3	4	5
15. Should show a thorough knowledge of their subject	1	2	3	4	5
16. Should show the relevance of their subject to work you expect to do when you qualify	1	2	3	4	5
17. Should point out the links between their subject and related subjects	1	2	3	4	5
18. Should be readily accessible to students outside formal classes	1	2	3	4	5
19. Should encourage students to express their own opinions	1	2	3	4	5
20. Should always be well prepared for their class	1	2	3	4	5
21. Should be punctual and reliable in attendance	1	2	3	4	5
22. Should try to link material to laboratory work/ practical work/fieldwork/seminars	1	2	3	4	5
23. Should be clearly audible	1	2	3	4	5

PLEASE MAKE SURE YOU HAVE ANSWERED ALL THE QUESTIONS

GENERAL LECTURE QUESTIONNAIRE

The purpose of this questionnaire is to obtain your views and opinions
about the lectures you have been given during the course from this
lecturer to help him evaluate his teaching.

Please ring the response that you think is most appropriate to each
statement. If you wish to make any comments in addition to those
ratings please do so on the back page.

The Lecturer	Strongly Agree	Agree	Neither Agree Nor Disagree	Disagree	Strongly Disagree
1. Encourages student participation in lectures	5	4	3	2	1
2. Allows opportunities for asking questions	5	4	3	2	1
3. Has a good lecture delivery	5	4	3	2	1
4. Has good rapport with students	5	4	3	2	1
5. Is approachable and friendly with students	5	4	3	2	1
6. Is respectful towards students	5	4	3	2	1
7. Is able to reach student level	5	4	3	2	1
8. Enables easy note taking	5	4	3	2	1
9. Provides useful printed notes*	5	4	3	2	1
10. Would help students by providing printed notes	5	4	3	2	1
11. Has a wide knowledge of his subject	5	4	3	2	1
12. Maintains student interest during lectures	5	4	3	2	1
13. Gives varied, lively lectures	5	4	3	2	1
14. Is clear and comprehensible in lectures	5	4	3	2	1
15. Gives lectures which are too fast to take in	5	4	3	2	1
16. Gives audible lectures	5	4	3	2	1
17. Gives structured, organised lectures	5	4	3	2	1
18. Appears to be enthusiastic for his subject	5	4	3	2	1

* Please answer if applicable

LECTURE FEEDBACK PROJECT

MAINTENANCE OF STUDENT INTEREST DURING LECTURES

The purpose of this questionnaire is to obtain your views on the way your lecturer maintains student interest during his lectures.

In Sections 1 and 2: Please ring the response that you think is the most appropriate to each statement.

Also in Section 2 please indicate by circling YES or NO whether or not you think the statement is a relevant one to ask. If you wish to make any comments in addition to these ratings please do so on the back page.

Section 1

In general:	Always	Sometimes	Hardly Ever	Never
Does the personality of a lecturer affect your interest in the lecture	4	3	2	1
Should a lecturer centre his lecture round his students and their needs	4	3	2	1
Do occasional digressions in lectures add interest	4	3	2	1

Section 2

The Lecturer:	Strongly Agree	Agree	Neither Agree Nor Disagree	Disagree	Strongly Disagree	Relevant Statement	
1. Maintains student interest through rapport	5	4	3	2	1	Yes	No
2. Makes use of humour to maintain student interest	5	4	3	2	1	Yes	No
3. Is patient in his delivery	5	4	3	2	1	Yes	No
4. Is less concerned about the syllabus and more concerned with student interest	5	4	3	2	1	Yes	No
5. Tries to involve students in the subject matter	5	4	3	2	1	Yes	No
6. Centres his lectures around students and their needs	5	4	3	2	1	Yes	No
7. Talks to the students and not AT them	5	4	3	2	1	Yes	No
8. Makes digressions which add interest	5	4	3	2	1	Yes	No

114909

		Strongly Agree	Agree	Neither Agree Nor Disagree	Disagree	Strongly Disagree	Relevant Statement	
9.	Produces a loss of interest due to his slow pace	5	4	3	2	1	Yes	No
10.	Gives dry formal lectures	5	4	3	2	1	Yes	No
11.	Reads straight from notes without pausing	5	4	3	2	1	Yes	No
12.	Has a monotonous voice which causes the mind to wander	5	4	3	2	1	Yes	No
13.	Gives varied lectures	5	4	3	2	1	Yes	No
14.	Has a good lecture delivery	5	4	3	2	1	Yes	No
15.	Makes lectures interesting and chatty	5	4	3	2	1	Yes	No
16.	Causes loss of interest through repetition	5	4	3	2	1	Yes	No
17.	Makes unexciting material bearable	5	4	3	2	1	Yes	No
18.	Maintains interest through clarity of explanations	5	4	3	2	1	Yes	No
19.	Confuses students	5	4	3	2	1	Yes	No
20.	Covers much new ground in lectures	5	4	3	2	1	Yes	No

Some further reading

On the nature of explaining

ENNIS, R. (1969) *Logic in Teaching*, Englewood Cliffs, N.J., Prentice-Hall. A thorough exposition of various types of explanation.

MARTIN, J. R. (1970) *Explaining, Understanding and Teaching*, New York, McGraw-Hill. For those with a penchant for logical arguments.

TAYLOR, D. M. (1970) *Explanation and Meaning*, Cambridge University Press. A clear introduction to the philosophical aspects of explaining.

On teaching explanations

THYNE, J. M. (1963) *The Psychology of Learning and the Techniques of Teaching*, University of London Press. An eminently readable and thoughtful book which provides useful logical analyses and hints rather than citations of numerous experiments. Chapter 7 deals with explaining; the other chapters are well worth reading.

On research on explanatory teaching

DUNKIN, M. J. and BIDDLE, B. (1974) *The Study of Teaching*, New York, Holt Rinehart. An extremely well-organised systematic account of researches on teaching which have used measures of pupil or student learning as one of their criteria.

WESTBURY, A. and BELLACK, A. (eds) (1972) *Research into Classroom Processes*, New York, Teachers' College Press. See particularly the chapter by Gage and his associates on their experiments on explaining.

On lecturing

BLIGH, D. (1972) *What's the use of Lectures?*, Harmondsworth, Penguin Books. Describes in detail research evidence on learning from lectures and lecturing and various methods of preparing and giving lectures. An invaluable work.

DUBIN, R. and TAVEGGIA, T. C. (1968) *The Teaching–Learning Paradox*, Center for Advanced Study of Educational Administration, University of Oregon. A thorough review but it uses the sole criterion of examination results to distinguish effectiveness of teaching methods.

McLEISH, J. (1976) The lecture method. In Gage, N. L. (ed.), *The Psychology of Teaching Methods*, Chicago, 75th Yearbook of the National Society
for the Study of Education. An up-to-date review which includes references
to Soviet and European work.

VERNER, C. and DICKINSON, G. (1968) The lecture, an analysis and review of
research. *Adult Education*, vol. 17 (winter), pp. 88–100. A very useful review
of research on lecturing up to the mid-1960s. Marred slightly by its messy
reference system which appears to have been designed to save space but
waste reader's time.

On helping students learn from lectures

MADDOX, H. (1970) *How to Study*, London, Pan Books. Practical hints on all
study techniques including note-taking from lectures.

REID, J. F. (1974) *A Guide to Effective Study*, University of Edinburgh, Transition Publication. A brief and helpful guide for the university student.

ROWNTREE, D. (1976) *Learn to Study*, 2nd ed., London, Macdonald and Janes.
A useful programmed text which contains hints on note-taking.

On teaching and research on teaching

BEARD, R. (1976) *Teaching and Learning in Higher Education*, 3rd edn, Harmondsworth, Penguin Books. An informed review of the whole field.

BLIGH, D., EBRAHIM, N., JAQUES, D. and PIPER, D. W. (1975) *Teaching
Students*, University of Exeter. A comprehensive survey of research findings
in higher education. An invaluable reference source. Also contains some hints
on teaching.

HEIM, A. (1976) *Teaching and Learning in Higher Education*, London, National
Foundation for Educational Research. A lively, personal account of teaching
and learning. Full of sound sense.

JACKSON, D. and JAQUES, D. (eds) (1976) *Improving University Teaching*,
University Teaching Methods Unit, University of London. A brief useful
survey of methods of teaching.

MACKENZIE, N., ERAUT, M. and JONES, H. C. (1976) *Teaching and Learning:
An Introduction to New Methods and Resources in Higher Education*, Paris,
UNESCO. A discussion of new methods and media in education.

TRENT, A. and COHEN, A. M. (1973) Research in higher education. In Travers,
R. M. W. (ed.), *Second Handbook of Research on Teaching*, Chicago, Rand
McNally. Deals primarily with the United States.

On various approaches to staff development and training

GREENAWAY, H. and HARDING, A. (in press) *Staff Development in Universities
and Polytechnics*, Society for Research in Higher Education, c/o University of
Surrey, Guildford. An updated account of training courses and staff development in British universities and polytechnics.

HARDING, A. and SAYER, S. (1975) The objectives of training university teachers. *Univ. Quarterly*, vol. 29, pp. 299–317. Discusses various approaches to training and development and advocates non-directive ones. Their views and mine do not always coincide. Worth reading and thinking about.

MILLER, G. W. (1976) *Staff Development Programmes in British Universities and Polytechnics*, Paris, International Institute for Educational Planning, UNESCO. A survey of programmes in use in 1974.

Society for Research in Higher Education (1977) *Staff Development in Higher Education*, S.R.H.E., c/o University of Surrey, Guildford. Report of the conference organised by the Society for Research in Higher Education.

University Teaching Methods Unit (1976) *Issues in Staff Development*, UTMU, University of London. A collection of papers; see particularly D. W. Piper's 'The longer reach'.

YORKE, M. (1977) Staff development in further and higher education: a review. *Brit. J. Teacher Education*, vol. 3, 2, pp. 161–9. Sets out three models of staff development and explores their implications for British higher education.

Journals and occasional publications

Assessment in Higher Education, ed. D. Harris, University of Bath.
Higher Education, ed. G. Williams, University of Lancaster/Elsevier.
Impetus, Newsletter of C.V.C.P., Co-ordinating Committee for the Training of University Teachers, ed. C. Matheson, University of East Anglia.
Studies in Higher Education, ed. A. Becher, University of Sussex/Carfax.
The Group for Research and Innovation in Higher Education of the Nuffield Foundation have produced several short publications. Full details are available from the Secretary, Nuffield Foundation, Nuffield Lodge, Regent's Park, London. Some of the publications are listed in the bibliography of this book. See, for example,

NUFFIELD FOUNDATION (1972–4) *Newsletters*, Group for Research and Innovation, in Higher Education (Nuffield Foundation, London).

NUFFIELD FOUNDATION (1974) *A Question of Degree, Assorted Papers on Assessment* (Nuffield Foundation, London).

NUFFIELD FOUNDATION (1975) *Supporting Teaching for a Change* (Nuffield Foundation, London).

Bibliography and author index

Page references for this book are shown in bold type. References without such page numbers were referred to when compiling this book and may be of interest to readers.

ADAMS, R. S. and BIDDLE, B. J. (1970) *Realities of Teaching: Exploration with Videotape*, New York, Holt Rinehart.

ARGYLE, M. (1967) *The Psychology of Interpersonal Behaviour*, Harmondsworth, Penguin Books. **23**

ARGYLE, M. (1970) *Social Interaction*, London, Methuen. **23**

ARGYLE, M. (1975) *Bodily Communication*, London, Methuen. **23**

ARIES, P. *Centuries of Childhood*, Harmondsworth, Penguin Books. **58**

BASSEY, M. (1968) Learning methods in tertiary education. Nottingham Regional College of Technology internal paper. **45, 101**

BEARD, R. (1976) *Teaching and Learning in Higher Education*, 3rd edn, Harmondsworth, Penguin Books. **90, 124**

BELLACK, A. *et al.* (1966) *The Language of the Classroom*, New York, Columbia University Press. **33**

BENNETT, D. J. and BENNETT, J. D. (1970) Making the scene. In Cosin, B. R. *et al.* (ed.) *School and Society: A Sociological Reader*, London, Routledge. **59**

BLACK, P. J. and RUTHERFORD, D. (1975) Evaluation studies of six courses in geography, electrical engineering and physics. In U.T.M.U. *Evaluating Teaching in Higher Education*, U.T.M.U., University of London, p. 102. **86**

BLIGH, D. (1972) *What's the Use of Lectures?*, Harmondsworth, Penguin Books. **41, 62, 123**

BLIGH, D., EBRAHIM, N., JAQUES, D. and PIPER, D. W. (1975) *Teaching Students*, University of Exeter. **41, 51, 90, 124**

BORG, W. (1975) Protocol materials as related to teacher performance and pupil achievement. *J. Educ. Research*, vol. 69, no. 1, Sept. 1975. **16**

BRADBURY, P. S. and RAMSDEN, P. (1975) Student evaluation of teaching at North East London Polytechnic. In U.T.M.U. *Evaluating Teaching in Higher Education*, U.T.M.U., University of London, pp. 94–101. **86**

BROUDY, H. (1963) Historic exemplars of teaching methods. In Gage, N. L. (ed.), *Handbook of Research on Teaching*, Chicago, Rand McNally, pp. 1–43.

BROWN, G. A. (1975) *Microteaching: A Programme of Teaching Skills*, London, Methuen.

BROWN, G. A. (1976) Using microteaching to train new lecturers. *University Vision*, vol. 15, pp. 24–31.

BROWN, G. A. and ARMSTRONG, S. (1977) S.A.I.D. System for Analysing Instructional Discourses. University of Nottingham, mimeo. 11, 33, 83

BROWN, G. A. (1978a) Techniques of explaining. University of Nottingham, mimeo.|17

BROWN, G. A. (1978b) Learning from lectures: a programme for students (sponsored by the Nuffield Foundation) University of Nottingham. 94

CANNON, R. and KAPELIS, Z. (1976) Learning spaces for higher education. *Prog. Learning and Educ. Technol.*, vol. 13, 2, pp. 13–24. 58

COATS, W. D. and SMIDCHENS, U. (1966) Audience recall as a function of speaker dynamism. *J. Educ. Psychol.*, vol. 57, 4, pp. 189–91.

COOPER, B. and FOY, J. M. (1967) Evaluating the effectiveness of lectures. *Univ. Quarterly*, vol. 21, pp. 182–5.

COSTIN, F. (1972) Lecturing versus other methods of teaching: a review of research. *Brit. J. Educ. Technol.* vol. 3, pp. 1–31. 41

DRESSEL, P. L. (1976) *Handbook of Academic Evaluation*, Amsterdam, Jossey Bass. 88

DUBIN, R. and TAVEGGIA, T. C. (1968) *The Teaching–Learning Paradox*, Centre for Advanced Study of Educational Administration, University of Oregon. 123

DUNCAN, C. J. (ed.) (1966) *Modern Lecture Theatres*, Sydney, Oriel Press.

DUNKIN, M. J. and BIDDLE, B. J. (1974) *The Study of Teaching*, New York, Holt Rinehart. 11, 16, 21, 123

EBEL, R. L. (1965) *Measuring Educational Attainment*, Englewood Cliffs, N. J., Prentice-Hall.

EGGLESTON, J., GALTON, M. J. and JONES, M. (1975) A conceptual map for interaction studies. In Chanan, G. and Delamont, S. (eds) *Frontiers of Classroom Research*, London, National Foundation for Educational Research. 32

EISNER, E. W. (1967) Educational objectives: help or hindrance? *School Rev.*, vol. 75, pp. 250–60.

ELTON, L. (1975) Can teaching be assessed? In U.T.M.U. *Evaluating Teaching in Higher Education*, U.T.M.U., University of London. 86

ENNIS, R. H. (1969) *Logic in Teaching*, Englewood Cliffs, N.J., Prentice-Hall. 9, 33, 123

ENTWHISTLE, N., PERCY, K. and NISBET, J. B. *Educational Objectives and Academic Performance in Higher Education*, University of Lancaster. 87

ERSKINE, C. and O'MORCHOE, C. (1961) Research on teaching methods: its significance for the curriculum, *Lancet*, vol. 1, pp. 709–11. 78

FANSLOW, W. W. (1965) Studies of attending behaviour. Doctoral thesis, Stanford University. 85

FLOOD-PAGE, C. (1974) *Student Evaluation of Teaching – The American Experience*, London, Society for Research into Higher Education, c/o University of Surrey, Guildford. 11, 86, 87

GAGE, N. L. (1972) in Westbury, I. and Bellack, A. (eds), *Research into Classroom Processes*, New York, Teachers College Press, ch. 9. 10, 11, 16

128 Bibliography and author index

GOHDIN, W. R., MANNEN, E. W. and DODDING, J. (1970) *The Art of Public Speaking Made Simple*, London, W. H. Allen. 25

GOLBY, M., GREENWALD, J. and WEST, R. (eds) (1975) *Curriculum Design*, London, Croom Helm/Open University. 90

GREENAWAY, H. and HARDING, A. (in press) *Staff Development in Universities and Polytechnics*, S.R.H.E., University of Surrey. 124

GROBE, R. P. and PETTIBONE, T. J. (1973) Effects of instructional pace on student attentiveness. Paper presented to Amer. Educ. Res. Assoc., New Orleans (Feb.). 85

GUYOT, Y. (1970) Teacher location of teacher–student relationships. *Int. Rev. Appl. Psychol.*, vol. 19, 2, 56–71. 60

HALL, W. C. (1975) *University Teaching*, Advisory Centre for University Education, University of Adelaide. 49, 88

HALLIDAY, M. A. K. and HASAN, R. (1976) *Cohesion in English*, London, Longmans. 48

HAMILTON, E. R. (1928) *The Art of Interrogation*, University of London Press. 84

HARDING, A. D. and SAYER, S. (1975) The objective of training university teachers. *Univ. Quarterly*, vol. 29, pp. 299–317. 125

HARTLEY, J. and CAMERON, A. (1967) Some observations on the efficiency of lecturing, *Educ. Rev.*, vol. 20, 1, pp. 30–7.

HARTLEY, J. and MARSHALL, S. (1974) On notes and note-taking. *Univ. Quarterly*, vol. 28, pp. 225–35. 45

HEMPEL, C. (1965) *Aspects of Scientific Explanation*, Glencoe, Ill., Free Press. 9

HERBART, J. F. (1893) *The Science of Education*, H. M. and E. Falkin. New York, Heath. 78

HEYWOOD, J. (1977) *Assessment in Higher Education*, New York, Wiley. 88

HILDEBRAND, M. (1973) The character and skills of the effective professor. *J. Higher Educ.*, vol. 44, 1, pp. 41–50.

HOWE, M. (ed.) (1977) *Adult Learning*, New York, Wiley. 45

HOWE, M. S. A. (1970) Using students' notes to examine the role of the individual in acquiring meaningful subject matter. *J. Educ. Res.*, vol. 64, 2, pp. 61–3.

JACKSON, D. and JAQUES, D. (eds) (1976) *Improving University Teaching*, U.T.M.U., University of London. 124

JOHNSON, H. C., RHODES, D. M. and RUMERY, R. E. (1975) The Assessment of teaching in higher education: a critical retrospect and a proposal. Part one: a critical retrospect. *Higher Education*, vol. 4, 2, pp. 173–99; Part two: a proposal, *ibid.*, vol. 4, 3, pp. 273–304.

JOHNSON, W. (1946) *People in Quandaries*, New York, Harper and Row.

JOHNSTONE, A. H. and PERCIVAL, F. (1976) Attention breaks in lectures. *Education in Chemistry*, vol. 13, pp. 49–50. 44

JONES, H. E. (1923) Experimental studies of college teaching. *Archives of Psychology*, vol. 68. 45, 101

KATZ, D. (1956) *Gestalt Psychology*, New York, Ronald Press. 78

Bibliography and author index 129

KING, M. (1973) The anxieties of university teachers. *Univ. Quarterly*, vol. 28, pp. 69–83. 42

KOHLAN, R. C. (1973) A comparison of faculty evaluations early and late in the course. *J. Higher Educ.*, vol. 44, pp. 587–595. 87

LAYTON, D. (ed.) (1968) *University Teaching in Transition*, Edinburgh, Oliver and Boyd. 57

LINDSAY, P. H. and NORMAN, D. A. (1972) *Human Information Processing*, New York, Academic Press. 44

LINN, R. L. and SLINDE, J. A. (1977) The determination of the significance of change between pre and post testing periods, *Rev. Educ. Res.*, vol. 47, pp. 121–50.

LLOYD, D. H. (1968) A concept of improvement of learning response in the taught lesson. *Visual Education*, 23–5 Oct. 44

MACDONALD-ROSS, M. (1973) Behavioural objectives: a critical review. *Instructional Science*, vol. 2, pp. 1–52. 91

MACGRAW, F. M. (1965) The use of 35mm time lapse photography as a feedback and observation instrument in teacher education. Doctoral thesis, Stanford University. 85

MCKEACHIE, W. J. (1963) Research on teaching at the college and university level. In Gage, N. L. (ed.), *Handbook of Research on Teaching*, Chicago, Rand-McNally, pp. 1118–72.

MACKENZIE, N., ERAUT, M. and JONES, H. C. (1970) *Teaching and Learning: An Introduction to New Methods and Resources in Higher Education*, Paris, UNESCO. 124

MCLEISH, J. (1968) *The Lecture Method*, Cambridge Institute of Education. 45

MCLEISH, J. (1976) The lecture method, in Gage, N. L. (ed.) *The Psychology of Teaching Methods*, Chicago, 75th Yearbook of the National Society for the Study of Education. 41, 101, 124

MADDOX, H. (1970) *How to Study*, London, Pan Books. 124

MADDOX, H. and HOOLE, E. (1975) Performance decrement in the lecture. *Educ. Res.*, vol. 28, pp. 17–30. 44

MAGER, R. F. (1962) *Preparing Instructional Objectives*, Palo Alto, Cal., Fearon. 91

MAIER, N. F. (1958) *The Appraisal Interview*, New York, Wiley. 112

MARTIN, J. R. (1970) *Explaining, Understanding and Teaching*, New York, McGraw-Hill. 123

MASTIN, E. (1963) Teacher enthusiasm. *J. Educ. Res.*, vol. 56, 7, 385–6.

MILLER, C. M. L. and PARLETT, M. (1974) *Up to the Mark*, Society for Research in Higher Education, c/o University of Surrey, Guildford. 60

MILLER, G. W. (1976) *Staff Development Programme in British Universities and Polytechnics*, Paris, International Institute of Educational Planning, UNESCO. 125

MILTZ, R. (1971) Development and evaluation of a manual for improving teachers' explanations. Doctoral dissertation, Stanford (available from the National Lending Library). 16, 21

NUFFIELD FOUNDATION (1972–4) *Newsletters*, Group for Research and Innovation in Higher Education, Nuffield Foundation, London. 125

NUFFIELD FOUNDATION (1974) *A Question of Degree, Assorted Papers on Assessment*, Nuffield Foundation, London. 125

NUFFIELD FOUNDATION (1975) *Supporting Teacher for a Change*, Nuffield Foundation, London. 125

N.U.S. (1969) *Report of the Commission on Teaching in Higher Education*, London, National Union of Students.

PEAR, T. H. (1933) *Psychology of Effective Speaking*, London, Routledge. 75

PERLBERG, A. (1976) The use of laboratory systems in improving university teaching, *Higher Education*, vol. 5, 2 (May).

REID, J. F. (1974) *A Guide to Effective Study*, University of Edinburgh, Transition Publication. 124

REMMERS, H. H. (1963) Rating methods in research on teaching. In Gage, N. L. (ed.), *Handbook of Research on Teaching*, Chicago, Rand-McNally, pp. 398–447.

RILEY, J. W., RYAN, B. F. and LIFSHITZ, M. (1969) *The Student Looks at His Teacher*, Rutgers University Press (1st edn, 1950). 87

ROBINSON, K. F. and BECKER, A. B. (1970) *Effective Speech for Teachers*, New York, McGraw-Hill. 25

ROGERS, C. *Freedom to Learn*, Indianapolis, Bobbs-Merrill. 112

ROSENSHINE, B. (1970) Enthusiastic teaching: a research review. *School Rev.*, vol. 78, pp. 499–516. Repr. in Morrison, A. and McIntyre, D. (eds), (1972) *The Social Psychology of Teaching*, Harmondsworth, Penguin Books. 16, 23

ROSENSHINE, B. (1971) *Teaching Behaviour and Student Achievement*, International Educational Achievement Studies No. 1, 3, 37 N.F.E.R. 16, 21

ROSENSHINE, B. and FURST, N. (1973) The use of direct observation to study teaching, in Travers, R. W. (ed.) *Second Handbook of Research on Teaching*, Chicago, Rand McNally, pp. 122–83. 32

ROWNTREE, D. (1974) *Educational Technology in Curriculum Development*, New York, Harper and Row. 52

ROWNTREE, D. (1976) *Learn to Study*, 2nd edn, London, Macdonald and Janes. 124

RYANS, D. G. (1961) *Characteristics of Teachers*, Washington, D.C., American Council on Education. 23

SHEFFIELD, E. F. (ed.) (1974) *Teaching in the Universities: No One Way*, McGill, Queens University Press.

S.H.R.E. (1977) *Staff Development in Higher Education*, Proceedings of Society for Research in Higher Education Conference, December 1977, S.R.H.E. c/o University of Surrey. 125

SINCLAIR, H. M. and COULTHARD, M. R. (1975) *Towards an Analysis of Discourse*, Oxford University Press. 33

SINGER, R. H. L. (1964) The use of manipulative strategies. *Sociometry*, vol. 27, pp. 128–51. 60

SMITH, B. O. and MEUX, M. (1970) *Study of the Logic of Teaching*, University of Illinois Press. 9, 33

SMITH, P. (1974) *The Design of Learning Spaces*, London, Council for Educational Technology. 58

SMITHERS, A. (1970a) Some factors in lecturing, *Educ. Rev.*, vol. 22, 2, pp. 141–50. 87

SMITHERS, A. (1970b) What do students expect of lectures? *Univ. Quarterly*, vol. 24, 3, pp. 330–6. 87

SOMMER, R. (1969) *Personal Space*, Englewood Cliffs, N.J., Prentice-Hall. 59

SPENCE, R. B. (1928) Lecture and class discussion in teaching educational psychology. *J. Educ. Psychol.*, vol. 19, pp. 454–62. 41

STUBBS, M. and DELAMONT, S. (eds) (1976) *Explorations in Classroom Observation*, New York, Wiley. 32

SWIFT, L. F. (1961) Explanation. In Ennis, R. H. and Smith, B. O. (eds), *Language and Concepts in Education*, Chicago, Rand McNally. 9

TAYLOR, D. M. (1970) *Explanation and Meaning*, Cambridge University Press. 123

TAYLOR, J. (1974) Design of educational building. *Brit. J. Educ. Technol.*, vol. 5, 3, pp. 4–12. 58

THYNE, J. M. (1963) *The Psychology of Learning and the Techniques of Teaching*, University of London Press. 7, 123

THYNE, J. M. (1974) *Principles of Examining*, University of London Press.

TRIBE, A. J. and GIBBS, J. (1977) Research in progress: analysing lecturing in low inference terms. *Res. Intelligence*, vol. 3, 3, pp. 32–6. 88

TURNEY, C. and CLIFT, J. C. *et al.* (1975) *Sydney Microskills Series 9*, Sydney University Press. 11, 16, 49

TYLER, L. (1969) A case history. In Popham, W. J. *et al.*, *Instructional Objectives*, American Educational Research Association Monograph 3, Chicago, Rand-McNally. 91

TYLER, R. W. (1954) *Basic Principles of Curriculum and Instruction*, University of Chicago Press. 91

VERNER, C. and DICKINSON, G. (1968) The lecture, an analysis and review of research. *Adult Education*, vol. 17, pp. 85–100. 124

WESTBURY, I. and BELLACK, A. (ed.) (1972) *Research into Classroom Processes*, New York Teachers' College Press. 123

WHITE, W. F. and WASH, J. A. (1966) Perception of teacher effectiveness as a function of students' need for approval. *Percep. and Motor Skills*, vol. 23, pp. 711–17. 87

WRIGHT, C. J. and NUTTALL, G. (1972) The relationship between teacher behaviours and pupil achievement in the experimental elementary science lessons. *Amer. Educ. Res. J.*, vol. 7, pp. 477–91. Repr. in Morrison, A. and McIntyre, D. (1972) *The Social Psychology of Teaching*, Harmondsworth, Penguin Books. 16, 21

YORKE, M. (1977) Staff development in further and higher education: a review. *Brit. J. Teacher Educ.*, vol. 3, 2, pp. 161–9. 125

Subject index